The Duck Commander Kitchen

– PRESENTS

CELEBRATING
FAMILY & FRIENDS

· · · · ·

Recipes for Every Month of the Year

KAY ROBERTSON

with CHRYS HOWARD

HOWARD BOOKS
An Imprint of Simon & Schuster, Inc.
NEW YORK   NASHVILLE   LONDON   TORONTO   SYDNEY   NEW DELHI

Howard Books
An Imprint of Simon & Schuster, Inc.
1230 Avenue of the Americas
New York, NY 10020

First Howard Books trade paperback edition April 2015

HOWARD and colophon are trademarks of Simon & Schuster, Inc.

For information about special discounts for bulk purchases, please contact Simon & Schuster Special Sales at 1-866-506-1949 or business@simonandschuster.com.

The Simon & Schuster Speakers Bureau can bring authors to your live event. For more information or to book an event, contact the Simon & Schuster Speakers Bureau at 1-866-248-3049 or visit our website at www.simonspeakers.com.

Interior design by Jaime Putorti

Manufactured in the United States of America

1 3 5 7 9 10 8 6 4 2

Library of Congress Cataloging-in-Publication Data

Robertson, Kay.
Duck Commander Kitchen presents Celebrating family and friends recipes for every month of the year /
Kay Robertson with Chrys Howard.
pages   cm
1. Cooking, American—Louisiana style.   2. Seasonal cooking.   3. Robertson, Kay—Family.   4. *Duck Dynasty* (Television program)
I. Howard, Chrys.   II. Title.   III. Title: Celebrating family and friends recipes for every month of the year.
TX715.2.L68R659   2015
641.59763—dc23   2014045574

ISBN 978-1-5011-1202-7
ISBN 978-1-4767-9573-7 (pbk)
ISBN 978-1-4767-9577-5 (ebook)

To my grandchildren and great-grandchildren

My grandchildren are my life. They bring me such a sense of purpose as I help to train them to love God and one another. It's especially fun to have so many granddaughters after having four rugged sons. Now I get to play dress up and baby dolls! Of course, my grandsons are just as special. I love seeing their daddies in them. What fun it has been to see the combination of my sons and their wives in their children. God creates each one of us differently, but it's great to see that He hands down some of the best traits—like dimples and a sense of humor. I love to cook for a full table and mine keeps getting bigger and bigger. Babies, grandbabies, great-grandbabies—it's the circle of life!

*Chrys and I love spending time
with all of our grandkids!*

Children's children are a crown to the aged,

and parents are the pride of their children.

—PROVERBS 17:6 NIV

Contents

Introduction

If you know anything about me, you know that I love to cook. It's something I learned from my grandmother, and to this day, I cherish the hours I spent with her in her kitchen. She taught me how to make the perfect piecrust and how to fry the juiciest chicken. But cooking wasn't the most important thing she taught me. She showed me the value of sharing what I cooked with others. My earliest memories of my life with Phil include cooking and sharing meals with our young friends and family members. I wouldn't trade those memories for anything.

I wrote this cookbook because I wanted to pass on to you my love for celebrating with friends and family every chance we get. It's been proven that families who share meals together—around a table, not in front of the TV—are happier and healthier in every way. Celebrating with others is never about the perfect place setting or the correct number of invited guests. My idea of "entertaining" is to open the screen door and say, "Y'all come on in!" This is probably not a shock to you, but I'm the party animal of the family. Phil would be quite content never to leave his house or his chair or his woods. But Phil understands and values relationships and has always stood next to me as we fried fish or baked a pie for guests who were looking for some biblical truth or marriage wisdom. He might go on to bed when he's done talking, but he never minds opening the door.

Sharing was a big part of cooking with my grandmother. We shared everything from cookies to brisket with church and community members who needed us to share in their celebration or their sadness. The occasions represented in this book provide year-long reasons to get together. From the pilgrims celebrating their year of good fortune to a young mom eager to open baby gifts, special occasions are the fabric of American society. I have never and will never claim to be the greatest cook in America, but I will claim to love cooking and love sharing what I cook.

In my first cookbook, I arranged the chapters around my family members and their favorite recipes. I hope you've had an opportunity to see it and cook from it. In this cookbook, I wanted to pass on to you our family's love of getting together and invite you to gather up your loved ones as often as you can. To help you do that, I collected a whole new set of recipes that are ideal for celebrating with the ones we love on holidays and gatherings for every month of the year.

I've included family favorites like black-eyed peas and Key lime pie for New Year's, chess pie and a wonderful ham for Easter, fried pickles and chicken-fried steak for Father's Day, and strawberry popsicles and lemonade chicken for the Fourth of July. I've added venison stew and pumpkin pie dip for Grandparents' Day (that's an under-celebrated day!), and I'll even teach you how to do a crawfish (or shrimp) boil that your family and friends will love! And of course, I've included some of the absolute best Thanksgiving and Christmas recipes, ranging from an amazing roast duck to a traditional turkey breast, along with candied yams, crab dip, and a fabulous pumpkin pie with brown-sugar whipped cream.

We Robertsons use any excuse we can to sit together around a table full of food and I encourage you to do the same. To help you do that, I've gathered recipes for every month of the year. Even though I've provided a menu for each month and a specific reason to get together, I hope you will be creative in mixing and matching these recipes to fit your tastes and preferences and to cook any time of the year you please.

Cooking isn't hard, but it does take time. As my grandmother would say, anything worth doing is worth doing right. So, find a recipe that fits with your lifestyle and your occasion and enjoy every minute of cooking it. Then sit back and watch those you cooked for laugh and talk and grow closer.

If you love to cook as I do, be grateful for that gift and enjoy exploring these recipes. If cooking isn't your favorite but you love to entertain, there are plenty of simple recipes in this book that I know you can do. Whatever you do, never underestimate the power of a perfectly timed casserole or fresh-baked cookies. They're always guaranteed to lift spirits and celebrate any occasion.

Like my first book, this cookbook is a dream come true. Thank you for being a part of my dream!

Miss Kay

New Year's Day

Celebrated on the First Day of January

■ ■ ■ ■ ■

And now we welcome the new year,

full of things that have never been.

—RAINER MARIA RILKE

God's loyal love couldn't have run out,

his merciful love couldn't have dried up.

They're created new every morning.

How great your faithfulness!

I'm sticking with God (I say it over and over).

—LAMENTATIONS 3:22–24 THE MESSAGE

Recipes for New Beginnings

It doesn't get much better than a homemade biscuit or muffin with a little (or a lot) of butter.

Celebrating New Beginnings

I love what the New Year stands for. When I was a young girl, all I ever wanted was a pioneer man to take care of me. I got that man, but not without a lot of grief during our first years of marriage. (You can read more about that in our other books.) For now, I just want to talk about the joy of starting over and, even more important, the joy of allowing others to start over. That's what a New Year stands for—new beginnings. Starting over is an amazing place to be!

Many years ago, a very prominent member of our home church came forward with a drug and alcohol problem. He was afraid to walk down the aisle and confess all the addictions that had controlled his life, but the result of his confession was overwhelming support and an attitude change in our entire church family. Since that time, our church family stands faithfully beside anyone who is ready to make a change in his or her life. I have seen drug addicts, thieves, adulterers, alcoholics, and more come to the front of our church and ask for help—and help is given. In my own life, I have had a husband and children who have taken the wrong path for a period of time. In those dark days, I had to depend on a lot of prayer, my church family, and the hope that I had in God and His saving grace.

In the book of Luke, Jesus tells the story of the Prodigal Son. This is one of my favorite "new beginnings" stories in the Bible. It's the story of a son who came to his father and asked to have his inheritance *now*. The father gave it to him, and as you might have guessed, the son blew the money on wild living and fair-weather friends. When life got hard and he had nowhere else to turn, the son decided to go home and beg his father for mercy. As he approached the old homestead, he saw that his father was on the road waiting for him. And when the son got in arms' reach, the father hugged and kissed him and called for a huge celebration.

I love the forgiveness that this father demonstrated. A forgiving spirit frees the offending person, but an unforgiving heart holds on to the grudge as tight as one of my dogs holds on to a bone. Letting go of the wrong done to us frees the offending person and it frees us. Letting go means we are letting God handle it and it is not ours to hold on to any longer.

So, it's a New Year! Time to do away with the old and bring in the new in many different ways. Celebrate new beginnings and let everyone around you do the same. Enjoy!

Warm Tomato-Cheese Dip

Makes 12 to 16 servings

1 pound regular or Mexican Velveeta, cut into ½-inch cubes

1 can (10 ounces) diced tomatoes and green chilies, such as Ro*Tel

Corn or tortilla chips, for serving

1. Place the Velveeta and tomatoes in a medium saucepan. Cook over medium heat until the cheese melts. Stir until the mixture is warm and well combined, about 5 minutes.

2. Serve warm with chips.

A younger Phil enjoying the great outdoors.

 *A Note from Miss Kay*

This is a favorite with the teens. This can also be done in your slow cooker and will last through the whole celebration.

Sausage Balls with Honey-Mustard Dipping Sauce

■ *Makes about 6 dozen*

Sausage Balls

2 rolls (16 ounces each) bulk
    breakfast sausage (I use Owens)
1 pound sharp cheddar cheese, grated
    (4 cups)
1½ cups baking mix, such as Bisquick
1 teaspoon onion powder
1 teaspoon garlic powder
¼ teaspoon black pepper

Dipping Sauce

½ cup Dijon mustard
½ cup yellow mustard
½ cup honey
½ cup mayonnaise
½ teaspoon cayenne, or to taste

1. For the sausage balls: Remove the sausage from the refrigerator 30 minutes before using.

2. Preheat the oven to 375°F.

3. In a large bowl, toss together the cheese, baking mix, onion powder, garlic powder, and pepper. Add the sausage and use your hands to knead it into the cheese mixture until the dry ingredients are moist and the mixture holds its shape when squeezed. This takes a while, so be patient and keep kneading. Refrigerate the mixture for 20 minutes.

4. For the sauce: Meanwhile, in a medium serving bowl, whisk together the Dijon, yellow mustard, honey, mayonnaise, and cayenne. Cover and chill until needed.

5. Form the sausage mixture into 1-inch balls. Working in batches, arrange the balls about 2 inches apart on a rimmed baking sheet. Bake until browned and a little crispy, 18 to 22 minutes. Serve hot with the sauce.

 *A Note from Miss Kay*

This is a party favorite for New Year's gatherings. Since my boys love all things meat, this is a great recipe for our family get-togethers. But watch out, because they go fast!

A Pot of Black-Eyed Peas

■ *Makes about 8 servings*

1 pound dried black-eyed peas

1 tablespoon bacon drippings or vegetable oil

1 large or 2 small ham hocks

1 medium onion, chopped (about 2 cups)

2 celery stalks, chopped (about 1 cup)

1 green bell pepper, diced (about 1 cup)

3 large garlic cloves, chopped

4 cups chicken broth or water, plus more as needed

2 sprigs (3-inch) fresh thyme

2 bay leaves

2 tablespoons apple cider vinegar

1 tablespoon salt, or to taste

½ teaspoon black pepper, or to taste

½ teaspoon cayenne, or to taste

 *A Note from Miss Kay*

Black-eyed peas are only one type of field pea. Try this recipe with others that you like, such as crowder peas or purple hull peas. This dish is a must on New Year's Day!

1. Place the peas in a large bowl and add cold water to cover by 3 inches. Let soak at room temperature overnight. Drain, rinse, and drain again. (For a quick-soak method, see p. 12, step 1.)

2. Heat the bacon drippings or vegetable oil in a large pot. Add the hock and sear until browned on all sides, about 1 minute per side. Remove from the pot and set aside.

3. Add the onion, celery, and bell pepper. Cook, stirring often, until tender, about 5 minutes. Add the garlic and cook 1 minute more.

4. Add the drained peas and enough broth or water to cover them by 1 inch. Return the ham hock to the pot and push down into the peas. Add the thyme and bay leaves.

5. Bring to a boil, reduce heat, partially cover, and simmer until the peas are almost tender, about 30 minutes. Make sure the top of the peas don't cook dry. Add more broth or water to keep them slightly submerged as they cook.

6. Stir in the vinegar, salt, pepper, and cayenne and continue simmering until the peas are tender and the liquid is thick and creamy, 10 to 20 minutes more. Discard the thyme sprigs and bay leaves.

7. Remove the hock and pull any meat from the bones (discard the bones). Finely chop the meat and stir into the peas. Check the seasoning and serve warm.

Tip: It's odd to think that dried peas and beans can get too old, but they can. If they don't get plump and tender enough to bite after soaking, then no amount of cooking will make them fully tender.

Texas Caviar

Makes 8 to 12 servings

2 cans (15 ounces each) black-eyed peas, drained and rinsed

½ small sweet onion, such as Vidalia, finely diced (about ½ cup)

2 Roma or plum tomatoes, seeded and finely diced (about 1 cup)

1 red bell pepper, finely diced (about 1 cup)

1 jalapeňo pepper, seeded and finely chopped

2 garlic cloves, finely chopped

¼ cup red wine vinegar

2 tablespoons extra-virgin olive oil

1 teaspoon hot sauce, or to taste

Salt and black pepper

¼ cup chopped flat-leaf parsley

Tortilla chips, for serving

1. In a large bowl, stir together the peas, onion, tomatoes, bell pepper, jalapeño, garlic, vinegar, and oil. Season with the hot sauce and salt and pepper to taste. Cover and refrigerate until chilled, at least 2 hours and up to overnight.

2. Stir in the parsley and check the seasoning before serving with the tortilla chips.

A Note from Miss Kay

I know this says Texas, but it's great in any state. New Year's Eve is the time to bring out the best dips and this is one of them!

"Red Beans" & Rice

Makes 8 servings

1 pound dried pinto beans (I use Camellia)

1 stick (¼ pound) butter

1 large onion, diced

12 ounces andouille sausage, cut into ¼-inch rounds (I use Savoie's)

2 tablespoons finely chopped garlic

1 box (2.4 ounces) Zatarain's Red Bean Seasoning Mix (see note for alternate)

1 large meaty ham bone or 2 ham hocks

10 cups chicken broth or water, plus more as needed

6 cups hot, freshly cooked long-grain white rice, for serving

Chopped green onions (scallions), for garnish (optional)

Hot sauce, for serving

1. Place the beans in a large bowl and add water to cover by 3 inches. Soak overnight. Drain, rinse, and drain again. (If you're in a hurry, you can quick-soak the beans: Pour them into a large pot, cover with water, and bring to a boil. Remove from heat, cover, and let sit 1 hour. Drain, rinse, and drain again.)

2. In a large pot or Dutch oven, melt the butter over medium-high heat. Add the onion and cook, stirring often, until tender, about 5 minutes. Add the sausage and cook, stirring often, until browned. Add the garlic and cook 1 minute more.

3. Stir in the drained beans and seasoning mix. Add the ham bone and push down into the beans. Add the broth. Bring to a boil, reduce the heat to medium-low, and simmer until the beans are tender and the broth begins to thicken, about 2 hours. If the top of the beans gets dry, add more broth to keep them barely covered.

4. Remove from the heat. Remove the ham bone (or hocks). Trim off any good meat (discard the bone), chop it, and return to the pot.

5. Serve hot with rice. If desired, garnish with chopped green onions. Pass a bottle of hot sauce at the table.

A Note from Miss Kay

We call this "red beans" because many people around here use red beans in this recipe, but my clan actually prefers pintos. Either type of dried bean works fine and tastes good. This recipe is full of great products that are easy to find here in West Monroe, but you might not find them in your grocery store. If that's the case, use any brand of pintos and andouille that you like. If you can't find Zatarain's Red Bean Seasoning Mix, replace it with 2 teaspoons salt, 1 teaspoon black pepper, 1 teaspoon dried thyme, 1 teaspoon hot sauce, 1 teaspoon Creole seasoning, and 1 bay leaf.

Pizza Monkey Bread

Makes 8 servings

¼ cup extra-virgin olive oil

1 tablespoon pizza seasoning or Italian herb blend

1 teaspoon garlic powder

2 cans (13.8 ounces each) refrigerated pizza dough (I use Pillsbury Classic Pizza Crust)

8 ounces sliced pepperoni

2 cups (8 ounces) shredded Italian blend or mozzarella cheese

1 cup finely grated Parmesan cheese

Warmed pizza sauce or marinara sauce, for serving

1. Preheat the oven to 350°F.

2. In a large bowl, whisk together the oil, pizza seasoning, and garlic powder.

3. With kitchen scissors or a sharp knife, cut the dough into 2-inch pieces. Add to the bowl and toss to coat.

4. Cut the pepperoni slices in half or quarters, depending on size. Add to the bowl with the dough. Add the Italian blend cheese and toss to mix well.

5. Transfer the dough into a 10- to 12-cup Bundt pan or tube pan. Drizzle any oil left in the bowl over the top.

6. Bake until the bread is browned and cooked through, 30 to 40 minutes. Let cool in the pan for 5 minutes and then turn out onto a serving plate. Sprinkle with the Parmesan and serve warm with the sauce.

 *A Note from Miss Kay*

You can buy fresh pizza dough in some grocery stores. If you prefer to use that instead of canned dough, you'll need 1½ pounds. Yummy!

Marinated Coleslaw

Makes 12 servings

1 large green cabbage, finely shredded (about 12 cups)

1 tablespoon salt

1 large red onion, halved and very thinly sliced (about 3 cups)

2 large carrots, coarsely grated

¾ cup apple cider vinegar

1 cup sugar

½ cup vegetable oil

2 teaspoons mustard seeds

2 teaspoons celery seeds

½ teaspoon black pepper, or to taste

1. Place the cabbage in a large colander. Toss with the salt. Sit the colander in the sink to drain for 1 hour.

2. Transfer the cabbage to a large bowl. Add the onion and carrots and toss to combine.

3. In a medium saucepan, combine the vinegar, sugar, oil, mustard seeds, celery seeds, and pepper and bring to a boil over medium-high heat, whisking until the sugar dissolves. Pour the hot vinegar mixture over the cabbage mixture and stir to coat. Let sit at room temperature for 1 hour, tossing occasionally.

4. Cover and refrigerate overnight. Toss well and check the seasoning before serving lightly chilled.

 *A Note from Miss Kay*

Not everyone in my family loves coleslaw, but for those who do, this is a great recipe, and one that can be done ahead of time. I love anything that has early prep time.

Our sons and their young families.

Here we are several years later—still growing!

Warm Ham & Cheese Party Rolls

Makes 1 dozen

1½ sticks (12 tablespoons) butter

¼ cup packed light brown sugar

¼ cup Dijon mustard

1 tablespoon Worcestershire sauce

2 teaspoons poppy seeds

2 teaspoons onion powder

Two 12-packs small potato rolls, slider buns, or Hawaiian rolls

Salt and black pepper

1 pound very thinly sliced deli ham

12 ounces thinly sliced provolone or Swiss cheese

1. Preheat the oven to 325°F.

2. Heat the butter and brown sugar in a small saucepan over medium heat, stirring until melted and smooth. Remove from the heat and stir in the mustard, Worcestershire sauce, poppy seeds, and onion powder.

3. Split the rolls in half horizontally. (Do not separate into individual rolls.) Spread the cut sides with two-thirds of the butter mixture. Season with salt and pepper to taste. Arrange the ham and cheese over the bottom halves of the rolls. Replace top halves of the rolls. Place in a 9 x 13-inch baking pan. Drizzle the remaining butter mixture over the tops. Cover with foil.

4. Bake for about 20 minutes to melt the cheese. Remove the foil and continue baking until the rolls are lightly browned, about 5 minutes more. Separate into individual rolls. Serve warm.

A Note from Miss Kay

The great thing about this dish is you can assemble these rolls and refrigerate them up to 1 day ahead before baking. That way you're ready for the party!

Slow-Cooker Pork Barbecue Sliders

■ *Makes 12 servings*

Cooking spray

1 large onion, thinly sliced

5 pounds boneless pork shoulder
 (Boston butt)

1 cup Coca-Cola (not diet) or dark
 beer

2½ cups bottled sweet, smoky
 barbecue sauce, divided, plus more
 as needed

4 garlic cloves, chopped

1 tablespoon packed dark brown
 sugar

2 teaspoons red pepper flakes

1 tablespoon salt

1 teaspoon ground cumin

½ teaspoon ground cinnamon

24 warmed slider-size sandwich buns

24 dill pickle slices

1. Mist the insert of a 6-quart slow cooker with cooking spray. Spread the onion over the bottom and place the pork on top.

2. In a medium bowl, stir together the Coca-Cola, 1 cup of the barbecue sauce, the garlic, brown sugar, pepper flakes, salt, cumin, and cinnamon. Pour over the pork.

3. Cover and cook on the low setting for 8 to 10 hours or until the pork is very tender. You should be able to easily pull off a piece of meat with tongs or a spoon. Remove the pork from the cooker and discard the cooking liquid and onions. Use two forks to shred the pork into bite-size pieces. Discard any large pieces of fat. Toss the shredded pork with the remaining 1½ cups barbecue sauce.

4. Serve the pork on warm slider buns. Drizzle with more barbecue sauce if desired. Garnish the tops with a dill pickle slice on a toothpick or put a slice inside the sandwich.

 *A Note from Miss Kay*

Phil loves a different brand of barbecue sauce than I do. I like Sweet Baby Ray's Honey Barbecue and Phil likes Smoky Cattlemen's, so you decide.

Key Lime Pie

■ *Makes 8 servings*

1 can (14 ounces) sweetened condensed milk, such as Eagle Brand

3 large egg yolks

½ cup bottled Key lime juice (I use Nellie & Joe's)

One 9-inch graham cracker crust

1 to 2 cups lightly sweetened whipped cream

1. Preheat the oven to 350°F.

2. In a large bowl, whisk together the condensed milk and yolks until smooth. Whisk in the juice until smooth. The mixture will thicken slightly. Pour the filling into the piecrust.

3. Bake for 15 minutes. Let pie cool to room temperature on a wire cooling rack. Cover and refrigerate until chilled, at least 4 hours and up to overnight.

4. Just before serving, top with the whipped cream.

All of the kids love ski vacations. It's a great way to start the year!

A Note from Miss Kay

Who doesn't like a great Key lime pie? Most people think it's really hard to make, but this one is so simple and delicious. Even my grandkids love it. Definitely give it a try!

Easy Chocolate Truffles

Makes about 3 dozen

3 cups semisweet chocolate chips

1 package (8 ounces) cream cheese, at room temperature

3 cups powdered sugar, sifted, plus about ½ cup for rolling

1 teaspoon vanilla extract

About ½ cup unsweetened cocoa powder, for rolling

1. Place the chocolate chips in a medium glass bowl. Microwave on 50% power in 30-second intervals until the chips begin to lose their shape. Stir until melted and smooth.

2. In a large bowl, with an electric mixer on high speed, beat the cream cheese until smooth. With the mixer set on low speed, beat in the powdered sugar 1 cup at a time, beating until smooth. Also on low speed, mix in the melted chocolate and vanilla. Refrigerate until the mixture begins to firm, about 45 minutes.

3. Use a tablespoon or small ice cream scoop to scrape up mounds of the chocolate. Arrange the mounds on a baking sheet and refrigerate until firm, about 1 hour.

4. Roll each mound in your palms to form a 1-inch ball. If the mixture is so cold that it crumbles, let sit at room temperature for a few minutes. Arrange the balls on the baking sheet.

5. Sprinkle about ½ cup powdered sugar on a plate. Sprinkle about ½ cup cocoa powder on a second plate. Roll half of the truffles in the powdered sugar until lightly coated. Arrange in a single layer on a serving plate. Roll the remaining truffles in the cocoa powder and arrange on the serving plate.

 *A Note from Miss Kay*

You can coat the truffles in other coatings of your choice, such as coconut, very finely chopped nuts, or sprinkles. These make a great gift. If you're really fancy, place each truffle in a paper candy cup or mini cupcake liner, then arrange them in a box or tin.

- 2 -

Valentine's Day

Celebrated on the Fourteenth Day of February

· · · · ·

Happy is the man who finds a true friend,
and far happier is he who finds that true friend in his wife.
—FRANZ SCHUBERT

Love never gives up.

Love cares more for others than for self.

Love doesn't want what it doesn't have.

Love doesn't strut,

Doesn't have a swelled head,

Doesn't force itself on others,

Isn't always "me first,"

Doesn't fly off the handle,

Doesn't keep score of the sins of others,

Doesn't revel when others grovel,

Takes pleasure in the flowering of truth,

Puts up with anything,

Trusts God always,

Always looks for the best,

Never looks back,

But keeps going to the end.

—1 CORINTHIANS 13:4–7 THE MESSAGE

Recipes for Those You Love

This man and I go way back!
He's always my Valentine.

Celebrating Love in Your Home

I love to decorate my house to celebrate any occasion. Once when the boys were young, I put hearts all over the house to celebrate Valentine's Day and didn't take them down for months. The boys had a friend over and he looked around the house and said in his teenage I-don't-get-it voice, "You guys have hearts hanging everywhere!" Yep, we did. Everywhere! Thinking back now, I hope that boy could see that not only did we have hearts hanging everywhere, we had—and have—*love* hanging everywhere.

It's sad, but we often show love everywhere *except* in our homes. We go to work and treat our coworkers better than we do those we truly love. Our kids go to school and treat their friends better than they do their siblings. Why is this true? Part of the reason is that home is where we can relax and let our guards down. Another reason is that our family signed up for life, so no matter what we say or do, we know they aren't going anywhere. The very things that make family special might cause us to yell, ignore, lash out, and complain about one another.

As parents, it's our job to model the kind of behavior we want our children to have. (Trust me, I understand that even with the best models, our children will do things we will be shocked at!) But it does have to start with us as parents. Phil and I have always tried to speak kindly and lovingly to each other. We have tried to create a home atmosphere that is pleasant to live in. With four boys, we also tried to create a home that is fun. I'm so blessed that my boys have inherited a sense of humor (for the most part). I say for the most part because we've had our battles over who's the best at just about everything from Scrabble tournaments to heated domino games. In the end, though, there was always lots to laugh at.

Another thing we did was we always welcomed our boys' friends into our home. We live pretty deep in the woods of northeast Louisiana, but somehow friends found their way to our house. Phil would include them in any Bible study he was doing while I would set another plate at the table. That's just how it was and still is. I hardly ever cook for just Phil and me. A big pot of something is on the stove at all times, ready for company. If you're reading this and you're not a cook, first of all thanks for buying my cookbook, but second, you don't have to be a big cook to open your home to others. Korie's mother (Chrys) is a self-declared noncook, but her home is always open to others. And she really does cook; she just doesn't love it like I do. But cooking is not the criteria to opening your home, opening your home is the criterion. Letting others know they are welcome is all you really need to do.

Creating a loving home and celebrating the love in your home is really easy. Just be good role models, keep the atmosphere pleasant and fun, and open the door!

Our family loves acting silly together—even at the airport!

Corn Pudding

Cooking spray

5 large eggs

½ cup heavy cream

5 tablespoons butter, melted and
slightly cooled

¼ cup sugar

¼ cup cornstarch

1 teaspoon salt

¼ teaspoon black pepper

1 can (15 ounces) whole kernel corn,
drained

1 can (15 ounces) cream-style corn

1. Preheat the oven to 400°F. Mist a shallow 2-quart baking dish with cooking spray.

2. In a large bowl, whisk the eggs until lightly beaten. Whisk in the cream, melted butter, sugar, cornstarch, salt, and pepper until smooth. Stir in the whole kernel corn and creamed corn.

3. Pour into the baking dish. Bake until just set, about 1 hour. Place a sheet of foil over the dish if top browns too quickly. Let sit 15 minutes before serving warm.

 *A Note from Miss Kay*

This is about the best corn you'll ever taste! And it goes with anything. Enjoy!

Mayonnaise Muffin Rolls

■ *Makes 1 dozen*

Cooking spray

2 cups self-rising flour

1 tablespoon sugar

¼ cup mayonnaise (not fat-free)

1 cup whole milk

1. Preheat the oven to 425°F. Mist 12 cups of a standard muffin tin with cooking spray.

2. In a large bowl, whisk together the flour and sugar. In a small bowl, whisk together the mayonnaise and milk. Pour the mayo mixture into the flour mixture and stir until blended.

3. Spoon the batter into the muffin cups. Bake until the rolls are golden brown, about 15 minutes. Serve hot.

 *A Note from Miss Kay*

Part roll, part biscuit, and part muffin, this is a quick solution for getting hot bread on the table. Love it!

Shrimp Cocktail with Rémoulade

■ *Makes 4 servings*

Rémoulade

¾ cup mayonnaise

1 tablespoon lemon juice

1 tablespoon horseradish, or to taste

½ teaspoon hot sauce, or to taste

¼ cup ketchup

1 tablespoon Creole mustard

2 green onions (scallions), finely chopped

1 teaspoon Creole seasoning, such as Tony Chachere's

1 teaspoon Worcestershire sauce

1 tablespoon drained capers

Shrimp

1 small onion, quartered

5 whole black peppercorns

1 bay leaf

1 tablespoon kosher salt

Juice of 1 lemon, halved

1 pound large (16/20 count) shell-on shrimp

Lemon wedges and ice cubes, for serving

1. For the rémoulade: In a medium bowl, stir together all of the ingredients. Cover and chill.

2. For the shrimp: Fill a large saucepan halfway with water. Add the onion, peppercorns, bay leaf, and salt. Squeeze in the lemon juice and drop in the halves. Bring to a boil over high heat. Reduce the heat and simmer for 5 minutes.

3. Remove from the heat, stir in the shrimp, cover, and let sit only until the shrimp are opaque, about 5 minutes. Drain and rinse under cold running water until cool enough to handle. (Discard the onion, peppercorns, bay leaf, and lemon.) Peel and devein the shrimp, leaving the tails attached.

4. Before serving, cover and refrigerate until chilled, at least 3 hours and up to overnight. Serve with the rémoulade sauce and lemon wedges on the side. Add a few ice cubes to keep chilled.

 *A Note from Miss Kay*

We love our shrimp in Louisiana. This is another great recipe that can and should be done the night before. If you're having a small dinner party (rare for us), this makes a great appetizer. If you're like us and have lots of people over, just double up on the recipe and enjoy!

Spinach & Strawberry Salad with Poppy Seed Dressing

■ *Makes 4 servings*

Dressing

½ cup white balsamic or white wine vinegar

½ cup sugar

½ cup vegetable oil

1 tablespoon very finely chopped shallot

¼ teaspoon paprika

¼ teaspoon mustard powder

1 tablespoon poppy seeds

Salad

4 lightly packed cups (9 ounces) prewashed baby spinach leaves

1 cup halved or quartered and hulled strawberries

¼ cup blanched, slivered almonds or chopped pecans, lightly toasted

1. For the dressing: In a medium bowl, whisk together the vinegar and sugar. Let sit 5 minutes and then whisk until the sugar dissolves. Whisk in the oil, shallot, paprika, mustard powder, and poppy seeds.

2. For the salad: In a large serving bowl, toss together the spinach and strawberries. Drizzle with enough dressing to moisten the leaves and toss well with tongs.

3. Divide among 4 serving plates, sprinkle with the almonds, and serve at once. Serve any remaining dressing at the table.

 *A Note from Miss Kay*

The key to greatness for this recipe is delicious strawberries. Fortunately, we can always get them at home. In the summer, I find them at the farmers' market. In the winter, in the grocery store.

Twice-Baked Potatoes

4 large russet baking potatoes, scrubbed and dried

1 tablespoon vegetable oil

2 tablespoons butter, at room temperature

¼ cup whole milk, warmed

½ cup sour cream

½ cup plus 2 tablespoons grated sharp cheddar cheese, divided

¼ cup plus 2 tablespoons bacon bits or crumbled crisp-cooked bacon

1 teaspoon salt, or to taste

½ teaspoon black pepper, or to taste

1 tablespoon thinly sliced green onions (scallions)

Paprika, for sprinkling

1. Preheat the oven to 400°F.

2. Pierce the potatoes in a few places with the tip of a sharp knife. Rub the skins lightly and evenly with the oil. Place the potatoes directly on an oven rack and bake until a knife pierces them easily and the skins are crisp, about 1 hour. Leave the oven on.

3. When cool enough to handle, slice off the top of the potatoes horizontally. Use a small spoon to gently scoop out the white flesh and place in a large bowl, leaving a ½-inch-thick shell. Scoop the flesh from the sliced potato tops into the bowl and then discard or nibble on the skins.

4. Crush the potato flesh with a fork or back of a large spoon. Add the butter, milk, and sour cream and stir vigorously with a wooden spoon until the butter melts. Stir in ½ cup of the cheese and ¼ cup of the bacon. Season with the salt and pepper.

5. Spoon the potato mixture into the potato shells. Sprinkle the tops with the remaining 2 tablespoons cheese, 2 tablespoons bacon, and the green onions. Dust the tops with paprika. Place the shells on a baking sheet and bake until the cheese bubbles and the potatoes are heated through, about 15 minutes. Serve hot.

A Note from Miss Kay

These potatoes go with anything or just by themselves. Korie's parents don't eat meat, so this is a main course for them, if you leave off the bacon. And if you have a big family like we do, just double or triple the recipe.

Cast-Iron Skillet Strip Steaks

Makes 4 servings

4 strip steaks (sometimes called New York strips), each about 1½ inches thick

4 teaspoons vegetable oil

2 teaspoons salt

½ teaspoon black pepper

1. Remove the steaks from the refrigerator 30 minutes before cooking to let them come to room temperature.

2. Heat a large cast-iron skillet over high heat for 5 minutes. A sprinkling of water drops should sizzle, turn white, and evaporate instantly.

3. Lightly brush both sides of the steaks with the oil and sprinkle with the salt and pepper.

4. Turn on the stove vent, if you have one. Place the steaks in the skillet. (If all the steaks don't easily fit in the skillet with space between them, cook two at a time.) Let cook undisturbed for 3 minutes. There will be some popping and hissing. Turn with tongs and cook the other side 3 minutes more for medium-rare.

5. Place the steaks on a cutting board or serving plates and let rest 5 minutes before serving. Serve whole or slice on the diagonal and fan onto the plate.

 *A Note from Miss Kay*

This is a favorite for all the guys and simple to make even if you're a new cook. Try it, I'm sure you'll like it!

Chocolate-Covered Strawberries

Makes 6 to 8 servings

16 ounces semisweet chocolate chips

2 tablespoons plus 2 teaspoons vegetable shortening, such as Crisco

24 large fresh strawberries, preferably with stems (about 1 pound)

1 cup white chocolate chips

1. Place the semisweet chips and 2 tablespoons of the shortening in a medium glass bowl. Microwave on 50% power in 30-second intervals until the chips begin to lose their shape. Stir until melted and smooth.

2. Line a baking sheet with parchment paper or wax paper.

3. Rinse the berries and pat dry with paper towels. Holding the berries by the stem end, dip the berries in the chocolate, letting any excess drip off. Place coated berries on the lined baking sheet. Refrigerate until the chocolate hardens, about 30 minutes.

4. Place the white chocolate chips and remaining 2 teaspoons vegetable shortening in a small glass bowl. Microwave on 50% power in 30-second intervals until the chips begin to lose their shape. Stir until melted and smooth. Pour into a heavy-duty zip-top plastic bag, squeeze out excess air, and close the bag tightly. Squeeze the chocolate to one corner of the bag. Snip off a tiny piece of the corner and use the bag as a pastry bag to drizzle white chocolate over the berries. If you prefer to not use the bag, drizzle the white chocolate over the berries off the tines of a fork. Refrigerate until the white chocolate hardens.

5. Serve the berries lightly chilled.

 *A Note from Miss Kay*

The vegetable shortening makes the chocolate a little glossier and easier to handle. This is a fun one to do with the kids or grandkids. It's easy and looks beautiful!

Cherry Yum Yum

3 cups graham cracker crumbs

1 stick (¼ pound) butter, melted

1 package (8 ounces) cream cheese, at room temperature

¾ cup sugar

1 teaspoon vanilla extract

1 container (12 ounces) frozen whipped topping, such as Cool Whip, thawed

2 cans (21 ounces each) cherry pie filling (I use Lucky Leaf)

1. In a large bowl, toss together the crumbs and butter. Press two-thirds of the mixture into the bottom of a 9 x 13-inch baking dish. Set aside the remaining crumbs.

2. In a large bowl, with an electric mixer on high speed, beat the cream cheese until smooth. Add the sugar and vanilla and beat until fluffy, about 3 minutes. Fold in the whipped topping with a rubber spatula.

3. Spread half of the cream cheese mixture over the crust. Top with the pie filling. Cover with the remaining cream cheese mixture. Sprinkle with the remaining crumb and butter mixture.

4. Cover with plastic wrap and refrigerate until well chilled, at least 4 hours and preferably overnight.

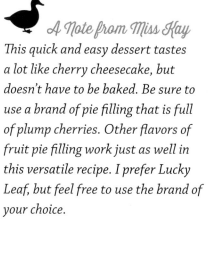

A Note from Miss Kay

This quick and easy dessert tastes a lot like cherry cheesecake, but doesn't have to be baked. Be sure to use a brand of pie filling that is full of plump cherries. Other flavors of fruit pie filling work just as well in this versatile recipe. I prefer Lucky Leaf, but feel free to use the brand of your choice.

Louisiana girls are always up for a ride in a golf cart.

Raspberry Spritzers

Makes 4 servings

Crushed ice

¼ cup raspberry flavoring syrup

2 cups cran-raspberry juice drink, chilled (see Tip)

2 cups lemon-lime soft drink, such as Sprite, chilled

Fresh raspberries and fresh mint sprigs, for garnish

1. Fill 4 tall drinking glasses half full with crushed ice. Or, if you want to be fancy, use pretty cocktail glasses. Spoon 1 tablespoon raspberry syrup into each glass. Add ½ cup juice and then ½ cup soft drink. Do not stir.

2. Garnish with the berries and mint and serve soon, before the soda loses its fizz.

Tip: Raspberry flavoring syrup is used in fancy coffee drinks, so look for bottles of it near the coffee in the grocery store. Torani is a common brand.

Jep, Jessica, and kids enjoying a relaxing day.

A Note from Miss Kay

For spritzers that are less sweet, use 100% cranberry-raspberry juice with no added sugar in place of the juice drink.

- 3 -

Wedding and Baby Showers

Celebrated Whenever Special Occasions Occur

■ ■ ■ ■ ■

The more you praise and celebrate your life,

the more there is in life to celebrate.

—OPRAH WINFREY

When Elizabeth was full-term in her pregnancy,

she bore a son. Her neighbors and relatives,

seeing that God had overwhelmed her with mercy,

celebrated with her.

—LUKE 1:57–58 THE MESSAGE

Recipes for Special Showers

I love preparing for parties with my daughters-in-law.
Their company makes everything more fun.

Celebrating with Others

Many people want to wait until their house is perfect or there's money in the bank before they decide to use their home to celebrate with others. But I'm here to tell you, don't wait. Celebrating the occasions of life is more important than whether or not your house is big enough or how much money you have in the bank. One of my favorite memories is when Phil and I were in college. My best friend was pregnant and I wanted to have a baby shower for her. We lived in the tiniest apartment and didn't have a spare dime to our names, but I was determined to celebrate.

I don't really know what Pinterest is, but I've heard the girls talk about it, and if I ever had a Pinterest moment, it was preparing for this baby shower. Everything was homemade. It had to be, we couldn't afford to buy anything. Somehow we even fashioned tiny baby diapers to hold peanuts. I can't remember exactly how we did it, but somehow we dipped our little diapers in wax and when they hardened, filled them with nuts. Hey, that's pretty creative for a seventeen-year-old with no Pinterest available!

My point is this: people are most concerned that you love them and want to celebrate with them than they are about everything being perfect. Over the years, I have had the honor of hosting many more showers and I'm pretty sure I never made little wax diapers again, but I have made cookies, decorated tables, brought gifts, and given out lots of hugs to happy new moms or brides. The Bible tells us to rejoice when others rejoice, so sharing in someone else's joy is a biblical concept. Everyone needs confirmation and support for what they are doing. Helping someone celebrate a milestone (this includes graduation, birthdays, anniversaries, etc.) tells that person that you are affirming their decisions and standing in support of them. That doesn't mean you have to go party-crazy. If your budget doesn't lend itself to a huge party, scale it down. No one said you have to serve an eight-course meal to celebrate. Invite friends over for cake and ice cream or have everyone bring something. That way everyone has the opportunity to bless others.

I'm sure you know this by now, but life can be challenging. Celebrating and honoring others when the occasion calls for it makes everyone happy, happy, happy.

The guest of honor was having twins!

Dill Snack Crackers

Makes 10 servings

¼ cup vegetable oil
1 packet (1 ounce) ranch dressing mix
½ teaspoon dried dill
½ teaspoon lemon pepper
½ teaspoon garlic powder
5 cups (9 ounces) oyster crackers

1. Preheat the oven to 250°F.

2. In a large bowl, whisk together the oil, dressing mix, dill, lemon pepper, and garlic powder. Add the crackers and stir until coated evenly with the oil mixture.

3. Spread the crackers on a rimmed baking sheet. Bake until golden brown, 15 to 20 minutes, stirring every 5 minutes. Cool to room temperature. Store in an airtight container at room temperature.

 *A Note from Miss Kay*

These crunchy little crackers make a great snack for nibbling, but they also make a fun crouton to sprinkle over soups and salads.

Asparagus Roll-Ups

Makes 4 to 6 servings

Cooking spray

½ teaspoon salt

12 thick asparagus spears, trimmed to about 5 inches long

8 ounces whipped cream cheese, at room temperature

¼ cup finely chopped crisp-cooked bacon or smoked ham

2 tablespoons finely chopped green onions (scallions)

12 slices very thin white sandwich bread, crusts removed

1 stick (¼ pound) butter, melted

¼ cup finely grated Parmesan cheese

1. Preheat the oven to 400°F. Mist a baking sheet with cooking spray.

2. Have ready a large bowl of ice water. Fill a large saucepan three-quarters full of water and bring to a boil. Then stir in the salt. Add the asparagus and cook for 1 minute. Move the asparagus immediately with tongs or a slotted spoon to the bowl of ice water. When cool, drain and pat dry.

3. In a small bowl, stir together the cream cheese, bacon, and green onions. Spread one side of each bread slice with the cream cheese mixture. Place an asparagus spear on one side of the bread and roll it up to form a cylinder that encloses the spear, leaving the tips exposed.

4. Generously brush the bread with the melted butter and roll in the Parmesan. Arrange the rolls on the baking sheet, seam side down, and bake until golden brown, 10 to 12 minutes. Serve warm.

 *A Note from Miss Kay*

If the asparagus is thin, you will need to use a total of 24 spears and place 2 in each roll.

Bite-Size Vegetable Quiches

■ *Makes 2 dozen*

Cooking spray
1 tablespoon butter
½ cup finely chopped red bell pepper
¼ cup chopped shallot
3 large eggs
1 tablespoon whole milk
1 tablespoon all-purpose flour
½ cup grated Gruyère cheese
½ teaspoon salt
⅛ teaspoon black pepper

1. Preheat the oven to 425°F. Mist a 24-cup mini muffin tin with cooking spray.

2. In a small skillet, melt the butter over medium-high heat. Stir in the bell pepper and shallot and cook, stirring often, until tender, about 5 minutes. Pour into a large bowl and let cool.

3. Whisk the eggs, milk, flour, Gruyère, salt, and pepper into the cooled vegetables.

4. Spoon about 1 tablespoon batter into each muffin cup. Bake only until the centers are set, 8 to 10 minutes. Let cool in the pan for 2 minutes. Loosen the edges with a butter knife and then remove from the tin. Serve warm.

Sharing in the wedding of Willie's best friend.

A Note from Miss Kay

Most showers have plenty of sweets. This is a great recipe for dieters or those who prefer a savory treat.

Spinach & Artichoke Dip in a Bread Bowl

Makes 16 servings

1 large round bread loaf, such as sourdough, rye, or pumpernickel

1 package (10 ounces) frozen chopped spinach, thawed

1 jar (12 ounces) marinated artichoke hearts, drained and coarsely chopped

¼ cup mayonnaise

½ cup sour cream

3 green onions (scallions), thinly sliced

2 tablespoons diced pimento, drained

1 can (4 ounces) sliced water chestnuts, drained

1 cup grated Parmesan cheese

1 cup grated Monterey jack cheese

1 teaspoon Old Bay seasoning

1 teaspoon hot sauce, or to taste

Crackers, for serving (optional)

1. Preheat the oven to 350°F.

2. Cut off the top third of the bread with a serrated knife. Use your fingers to pull out the soft interior, leaving a ½-inch-thick bread bowl. Set the bread bowl aside.

3. Cut the sliced-off top and the interior pieces of bread into 1-inch cubes. Spread the cubes on a rimmed baking sheet and bake until the outsides of the cubes are a little crisp, but the insides remain soft, about 8 minutes. Set the bread cubes aside to cool. Leave the oven on and place the bread bowl on the baking sheet.

4. Use your hand to squeeze small handfuls of thawed spinach as dry as possible. Shake the spinach loose into a large bowl.

5. Stir in the artichokes, mayonnaise, sour cream, green onions, pimento, water chestnuts, Parmesan, Monterey jack, Old Bay, and hot sauce and mix well.

6. Spoon the spinach mixture into the bread bowl. Bake until golden brown on top and heated through, 20 to 25 minutes. Serve warm with the toasted bread cubes and, if needed, extra crackers.

 *A Note from Miss Kay*

This is a favorite at every shower! You won't have (or get) to bring any home with you.

Strawberry Shortcake

Strawberries

1½ pounds strawberries, capped and
    halved or quartered
½ cup sugar

Shortcake

2 cups all-purpose flour
2 teaspoons baking powder
½ teaspoon baking soda
2 tablespoons sugar
¾ teaspoon salt
1½ cups heavy cream

Cream

1½ cups whipping cream, chilled
¼ cup powdered sugar
2 teaspoons vanilla extract

1. For the strawberries: In a large bowl, stir together the berries and sugar. Let sit at room temperature until the berries release some juice, stirring occasionally.

2. For the shortcake: Preheat the oven to 400°F. In a large bowl, whisk together the flour, baking powder, baking soda, sugar, and salt. Add the cream and stir with a fork to form a stiff dough. Scrape into an ungreased 8-inch square baking pan and pat gently to level the top. Bake until golden brown, about 20 minutes. Turn out onto a wire cooling rack and cool to room temperature.

3. For the cream: In a large chilled bowl, with an electric mixer (and chilled beaters), beat the cream, powdered sugar, and vanilla until stiff peaks form. Refrigerate until needed.

4. To assemble, split the shortcake horizontally in half with a serrated knife. Place the bottom half on a serving plate. Top with half of the whipped cream. Spoon two-thirds of the berries over the cream. Top with the other half of shortcake. Top with the remaining whipped cream and berries. Cut into pieces and serve immediately.

 A Note from Miss Kay

This shortcake recipe might take a little longer than just doing a cake mix, but it's well worth it. Delicious!

Cheese Coins

Makes about 8 dozen

3 sticks (¾ pound) butter, at room
    temperature
1 pound freshly grated sharp or
    extra-sharp yellow cheddar cheese
    (4 cups)
1½ teaspoons salt
½ teaspoon cayenne, or to taste
½ teaspoon paprika
4 cups all-purpose flour

1. Preheat the oven to 350°F. Line a rimmed baking sheet with parchment paper.

2. Place the butter, cheese, salt, cayenne, and paprika in a food processor (see Tip). Pulse to combine. Add 2 cups of the flour and pulse to combine. Add the remaining 2 cups flour and pulse until large clumps of dough form. Pour the clumps onto a large sheet of parchment paper and gather into a ball. Cover with a second sheet of parchment paper and roll to ¼-inch thickness. Refrigerate for 20 minutes.

3. Stamp out cheese coins with a 1½-inch round cutter. Place the coins on lined baking sheet, spacing them about 1 inch apart. Gather any scraps of dough, re-roll, and cut more coins.

4. Bake until just firm and light golden brown, about 12 minutes. Cool in the pan for 5 minutes, then transfer to a wire cooling rack to cool to room temperature. Store at room temperature in an airtight container.

Tip: If you don't have a food processor, mix the dough in a bowl of a heavy-duty stand mixer. Or, if you have only a hand mixer, divide the ingredients in half and make two smaller batches of dough. Also you can cut the dough into squares or strips with a pizza cutter or sharp knife, if you prefer.

 *A Note from Miss Kay*

Be sure to grate the cheese just before adding it to the dough. You might be tempted to get the pregrated packaged cheese, but it doesn't work as well in this recipe.

Curried Shrimp Salad Tea Sandwiches

Makes 18 sandwiches

1 package (8 ounces) cream cheese, at room temperature

½ cup mayonnaise

1 tablespoon lemon juice

1 teaspoon ground ginger

1½ teaspoons curry powder

¼ teaspoon salt

3 tablespoons finely chopped green onions (scallions)

½ cup finely diced celery

1 cup finely diced unpeeled red apple

2½ cups finely chopped peeled and deveined cooked shrimp (about 1 pound)

36 slices thin white sandwich bread

1. In a large bowl, stir together the cream cheese, mayonnaise, lemon juice, ginger, curry powder, and salt until smooth. Fold in the green onions, celery, apple, and shrimp with a rubber spatula.

2. Spread the shrimp mixture on one side of 18 bread slices and top with the remaining bread slices. Trim the crusts from the sandwiches with a serrated knife. Cut each sandwich diagonally into two triangles. Serve soon or store in an airtight container in the refrigerator for up to 3 hours.

 *A Note from Miss Kay*

It's much easier to remove bread crusts after the sandwiches are made. They will cut more evenly and cleanly.

Brown Sugar Cookie Bites

■ *Makes about 5 dozen*

1 cup vegetable shortening
2 cups packed light brown sugar
2 large eggs, at room temperature
½ cup buttermilk
3½ cups all-purpose flour
1 teaspoon baking soda
1 teaspoon salt

1. In a large bowl, with an electric mixer on high speed, beat the shortening, brown sugar, and eggs until light and fluffy, about 3 minutes. Beat in the buttermilk on low speed.

2. In a medium bowl, whisk together the flour, baking soda, and salt. Add to the shortening mixture and beat on low speed only until the flour disappears.

3. Cover the dough and refrigerate for 1 hour.

4. Preheat the oven to 400°F. Lightly grease 2 rimmed baking sheets.

5. Drop the dough by rounded teaspoons onto the baking sheets. The cookies won't spread much, so you can place them fairly close together. Bake until browned and almost firm, 10 to 12 minutes. Cool in the pans to room temperature. The cookies continue to firm as they cool. Store at room temperature in an airtight container.

 *A Note from Miss Kay*

This is an easy dessert or snack for the kids after school or anytime. Don't tell them you used buttermilk. They will never know!

Sparkling Party Punch with Fruited Ice Ring

■ *Makes about 3½ quarts*

Ice Ring

Cooking spray
1 orange, cut into thin rounds
1 lemon, cut into thin rounds
1 lime, cut into thin rounds
12 maraschino cherries

Punch

3 cans (12 ounces each) frozen yellow
   or pink lemonade concentrate,
   thawed
4 cups pineapple juice, chilled
2 cups cold water
4 cups ginger ale, chilled

1. For the ice ring: Mist the inside of a 5-cup ring mold with cooking spray. Use a very light touch so that the frozen ring won't look greasy when unmolded. Arrange the orange, lemon, and lime slices and cherries in the mold. Add enough water to come halfway up the sides of the fruit (about 1 cup). Freeze until the water is solid and then fill the mold to the rim with more cold water. Freeze until firm. When ready to serve, quickly dip the bottom of the mold in hot water. Cover the mold with a large plate, hold them firmly together, and flip over. The ice ring should drop out of the mold.

2. For the punch: In a punch bowl, stir together the lemonade concentrate, pineapple juice, and cold water.

3. Just before serving, add the ginger ale and ice ring. Serve soon, while still bubbly.

 *A Note from Miss Kay*

All my daughters-in-law host many showers for our church family. It's rare that I'm asked to bring punch because they usually want me to cook, but this is a great punch if you need one.

Candied Pecans

Makes about 3 cups

¾ cup sugar

1 teaspoon apple pie or pumpkin pie spice

1 teaspoon salt

1 egg white

1 tablespoon water

3 cups pecan halves

1. Preheat the oven to 250°F. Line a rimmed baking sheet with foil.

2. In a small bowl, stir together the sugar, pie spice, and salt.

3. In a medium bowl, whisk together the egg white and water until frothy. Add the pecans and stir until coated. Sprinkle the sugar mixture over the pecans and toss to coat.

4. Spread the nuts on the lined baking sheet and bake, stirring every 15 minutes, until the coating dries and the pecans are crisp, about 1 hour. Cool to room temperature, stirring occasionally to break apart any clumps. Store at room temperature in an airtight container.

Lisa helped me host a baby shower for a good friend.

A Note from Miss Kay

We are surrounded by pecan orchards in northeast Louisiana, so there's never a shortage. This is quick and easy to make and the nut lovers at the party will thank you.

- 4 -

Easter

Celebrated on the First Sunday After the First Full Moon

■ ■ ■ ■ ■

Believers, look up—take courage.
The angels are nearer than you think.

—BILLY GRAHAM

Now faith is confidence in what we hope for

and assurance about what we do not see.

This is what the ancients were commended for.

By faith we understand that the universe

was formed at God's command,

so that what is seen was

not made out of what was visible.

—HEBREWS 11:1–3 NIV

Recipes for Easter Sunday

Missy and Mia at our Easter celebration.

Celebrating Your Faith

Easter is a special time for our family. We get together at Korie's mom's (Chrys's) house for a fabulous lunch followed by an enormous Easter egg hunt. Each family member contributes to the lunch, so there is a variety of food from the traditional sweet potatoes and ham to the three-layer cake with coconut-covered fluffy white icing from Mamaw Jo (Chrys's mom). While the "grandparent generation" gets the food ready, the "parent generation" hides the eggs. It's fun to see our older "kids" scrambling all over the yard trying to find a spot for close to five hundred eggs. I think they have as much fun as the little kids. After lunch, we all gather on Chrys's large, Southern-style front porch and, after someone yells "Go," watch the kids run through the yard collecting their eggs. We entice the older kids to hunt by putting money or movie bucks in some of the eggs. Of course lots of family pictures are taken and everyone has the best time.

As much fun as the lunch and egg hunt are, we all know and celebrate the true meaning of Easter. Easter is a holiday because someone decided the resurrection of Jesus is worth celebrating. We think so, too! Most people know by now that we have a strong faith in God and His resurrected son, Jesus. Yes, our family motto is faith, family, ducks—in that order—and we mean it! We start every Easter Sunday at church service. Like many churches, our church usually does something different on Easter. One time they asked Phil to play John the Baptist (you can see why, I'm sure), and he came in from the back of the church yelling his lines and scared the kids in the back rows! I'm not so sure they enjoyed his performance, but I don't think they will forget who John the Baptist was.

The Bible says that faith is hope in something we cannot see. When you think about it, all of us go through each day using faith. We have faith that our washing machine will work when we decide it's time to wash clothes. We have faith that our car will start when we put the key in the ignition. We have faith that the vitamins we take will actually improve our health.

I have faith in God, too. I see evidence of His handiwork when I walk through my yard that is covered in flowers and trees and when I look out on the magnificent lake that has been Phil's work and play area for more than sixty years. I see God when I think about my first grandbaby weighing a little less than two pounds when she was born, yet she survived and is now the mother of three daughters. I see God when I think back to the man Phil once was and a marriage that almost didn't make it. Now, with God's help, we have been married more than fifty years. These things are more real and believable to me than my car starting or my vitamins working.

Our faith can grow just by paying attention to what God is doing. When we do, we discover that evidences for faith are right there in front of us.

Great-granddaughter Bailey is ready for the hunt!

Buttery Mini Muffin Biscuits

Makes 2 dozen

Cooking spray

2 cups self-rising flour

2 sticks (½ pound) butter, at room temperature

1 cup sour cream (not nonfat)

1. Preheat the oven to 400°F. Mist a 24-cup mini muffin tin with cooking spray.

2. In a large bowl, stir together the flour and butter. Stir in the sour cream.

3. Place rounded tablespoons of dough into each muffin cup. Bake until golden brown, about 15 minutes. Serve hot.

 *A Note from Miss Kay*

These little biscuits are tender, foolproof, and perfect for beginning bakers. My family loves biscuits! This is a recipe even the littlest cooks can help with.

Peach Iced Tea

Makes 2½ quarts

1 cup water

1 cup sugar

6 cups freshly brewed ice tea

2 cups peach nectar

1 teaspoon almond extract

2 to 3 ripe peaches, peeled and cut into thin wedges, for garnish

1. In a small saucepan, bring the water and sugar to a boil, stirring until the sugar dissolves. Set aside to cool.

2. Pour the tea, peach nectar, and almond extract into a large serving pitcher. Sweeten to taste with the cooled sugar syrup.

3. Refrigerate until chilled. Serve over ice, garnished with sliced peach wedges.

 *A Note from Miss Kay*

The first step in this recipe is to make a sugar syrup (also called simple syrup). You can do this with any iced tea if you like it sweetened. It just makes dissolving easier. We love our iced tea in Louisiana. This recipe is for special occasions.

Herbed Deviled Eggs

Makes 6 to 8 servings

1 dozen large eggs
2 tablespoons mayonnaise
1 tablespoon yellow mustard
1 tablespoon finely chopped fresh chives
1 teaspoon finely chopped fresh dill
1 teaspoon salt, or to taste
¼ teaspoon ground white pepper, or to taste
24 pretty flat-leaf parsley leaves

1. Place the eggs in a single layer in a large saucepan. Cover with cold water. Bring to a boil over medium-high heat. As soon as the water begins to boil, remove the pan from the heat, cover, and let stand 10 minutes. Drain off the hot water and cover the eggs with ice water. Let sit until the eggs are cool enough to handle.

2. Peel the eggs under cold running water. Halve lengthwise, and place the egg yolks in a medium bowl. Arrange the egg whites on a serving platter.

3. Mash the yolks with a fork. Stir in the mayonnaise, mustard, chives, and dill. Season with the salt and white pepper.

4. Using a spoon, fill the egg whites with the yolk mixture. Garnish each with a parsley leaf. Cover and refrigerate until chilled.

 *A Note from Miss Kay*

I've found that eggs that are at least one week old are easier to peel cleanly. Deviled eggs (any recipe) never last long on our Easter table. This one will be gobbled up quickly!

Pecan Rice

■ *Makes 6 servings*

3 tablespoons butter or bacon grease

½ cup finely chopped onion

1½ cups long-grain white rice

1 cup chicken broth

1 cup water

1 teaspoon salt

¼ cup chopped pecans

2 tablespoons finely chopped flat-leaf parsley

1. In a large saucepan with a lid, melt the butter. Add the onion and cook, stirring often, until tender, about 5 minutes.

2. Add the rice and stir to coat. Add the broth, water, and salt. Bring to a boil, stir once, reduce the heat, cover, and simmer over medium-low heat for 15 minutes.

3. Remove from the heat and let sit, covered, for 10 minutes.

4. Fluff the rice with a fork and stir in the pecans and parsley. Check the seasoning. Serve warm.

The Easter gang ready for the hunt.

 *A Note from Miss Kay*

Rice can be a good addition to any meal. This recipe gives rice a different twist. The key to fluffy rice is to not lift the lid or stir while it's cooking and resting. Then use a fork to fluff it once it's done.

Brown Sugar–Crusted Baked Ham

■ *Makes 12 to 16 servings*

1 (8-pound) semi-boneless fully cooked ham

1 cup grainy Dijon mustard

1 to 1½ cups packed light brown sugar

1 bottle (12 ounces) Coca-Cola, preferably sweetened with cane sugar (not diet)

1 jar (12 ounces) pineapple preserves (I use Smucker's)

1. Preheat the oven to 325°F.

2. Remove the ham from wrapper. If the fat cap is still on the ham, trim it down to a ¼-inch thickness. Place the ham in a large, sturdy roasting pan.

3. Spread the mustard thickly over the top and sides of the ham. Cover the mustard with a crust of brown sugar, pressing it with the palm of your hand to help it adhere. Pour the cola into the bottom of the pan.

4. Roast until an instant-read thermometer inserted into the center without touching the bone registers 140°F, about 2 hours (15 minutes per pound). Let sit for 30 minutes before carving. Carefully pour the pan juices into a small saucepan. Stir in the preserves and cook over medium heat until the preserves melt.

5. Serve the ham drizzled with the pineapple preserve mixture.

 *A Note from Miss Kay*

A baked ham is the perfect centerpiece for Easter lunch, and it's easy to make. If you go with a large ham and don't have the crowds we have for Sunday lunch, you'll have plenty of leftovers: ham sandwiches, ham salad, and omelets. You could wrap it tightly and freeze it as well. I love using a leftover ham for fried ham, biscuits, and eggs!

Snap Beans with New Potatoes

Makes 8 servings

4 ounces bacon, chopped

Extra-virgin olive oil, as needed

1 medium onion, finely chopped
(about 2 cups)

3 pounds fresh green beans (see
Note)

1 tablespoon salt, or to taste

1 teaspoon black pepper, plus more
to taste

1 teaspoon garlic powder

3 cups chicken broth, plus more as
needed

12 small red potatoes, scrubbed,
halved (or quartered if larger than
a golf ball)

2 tablespoons butter

1. Cook the bacon in a large pot over medium-high heat until the fat renders and the bacon begins to brown, about 5 minutes. If the bacon produces less than 4 tablespoons of fat, add olive oil to make up the difference. Stir in the onion and cook, stirring occasionally, until tender, about 5 minutes.

2. Trim the ends of the beans, remove any tough strings, and snap the beans into bite-size lengths. Add the beans, salt, pepper, and garlic powder to the pan. Pour in enough broth to cover. Bring to a boil, reduce the heat, cover, and simmer until the beans are almost tender, about 25 minutes.

3. Stir in the potatoes and more chicken broth if the beans are almost dry. Partially cover and simmer until the vegetables are very tender, about 20 minutes more.

4. Stir in the butter. Check the seasoning. Serve warm.

 *A Note from Miss Kay*

This recipe tastes best when made with old-fashioned green beans that must have their ropey strings removed. Those tiny green beans that are often labeled haricots verts will turn to mush in this recipe. If you can't find the right kind of fresh green beans, use frozen Italian-style green pole beans, such as those from Pictsweet.

Garden Pea & Radish Salad

■ *Makes 6 to 8 servings*

1 cup mayonnaise

1 tablespoon sugar

½ teaspoon mustard powder

1 teaspoon salt, or to taste

¼ teaspoon black pepper, or to taste

1 bag (20 ounces) frozen baby green
   peas, thawed

½ cup thinly sliced radishes

4 ounces sharp cheddar or mozzarella
   cheese, cut into small cubes

1 cup cashews

1. In a large bowl, whisk together the mayonnaise, sugar, mustard powder, salt, and pepper. Let sit 5 minutes and then whisk until the sugar dissolves.

2. Add the peas, radishes, and cheese, stirring to coat. Cover and refrigerate until lightly chilled. Just before serving, stir in the cashews and check the seasoning.

The teens are giving us their "cool" looks after finding the coveted money eggs.

 *A Note from Miss Kay*

I know radishes aren't everyone's favorite, but they're delicious in this salad. I promise someone at your Easter table will love them.

Asparagus & Egg Casserole

Makes 8 servings

1½ to 2 pounds fresh asparagus, tough ends snapped off, spears cut into 2-inch lengths

4 hard-cooked eggs (see Tip)

½ stick (4 tablespoons) butter

2 tablespoons all-purpose flour

1 cup whole milk

½ teaspoon mustard powder

¼ teaspoon ground white pepper

½ teaspoon salt

½ cup grated Gruyère cheese

½ cup crushed buttery cracker crumbs, such as Ritz

1. Preheat the oven to 350°F. Butter a 9 x 13-inch baking dish.

2. Have ready a bowl of ice water. Bring a large saucepan of water to a boil. Add the asparagus and cook until crisp-tender, 1 to 2 minutes. Immediately transfer to the ice water with a slotted spoon. When cool, drain, and pat dry. Spread the asparagus in the bottom of the baking dish.

3. Coarsely chop the eggs and sprinkle over the asparagus.

4. In a medium saucepan, melt 2 tablespoons of the butter over medium-high heat. Whisk in the flour and cook, whisking constantly, for 2 minutes. Whisk in the milk and cook, whisking constantly, until the sauce thickens and bubbles, about 3 minutes. Remove from the heat and whisk in the mustard powder, pepper, salt, and Gruyère, whisking until smooth. Pour over the asparagus and eggs.

5. In a small saucepan, melt the remaining 2 tablespoons butter. Toss the cracker crumbs with the melted butter in a small bowl. Sprinkle over the top of the asparagus and eggs.

6. Bake until golden brown and bubbling around the edges of the dish, about 30 minutes. Serve warm.

Tip: To hard cook an egg, as opposed to hard boiling: Place the eggs in a deep saucepan, covering by 1 inch with cold water. Bring the water to a boil over high heat. Remove from the heat, cover, and let stand for 14 minutes. Transfer to a bowl of ice-cold water and allow to cool completely.

A Note from Miss Kay

For our family, we celebrate Easter at lunchtime, but many have an Easter breakfast or brunch. This casserole is perfect for either.

Coconut Layer Cake

■ *Makes 16 servings*

Cake

1 box French vanilla cake mix
Ingredients listed on cake mix
    package for preparing batter
½ teaspoon vanilla extract
¼ teaspoon coconut extract

Filling

2 cups sugar
2 cups sour cream
1 bag (14 ounces) sweetened flaked
    coconut (about 5⅓ cups), such as
    Baker's Angel Flake

Frosting

4 sticks (1 pound) unsalted butter, at
    room temperature
5 to 6 cups powdered sugar, sifted
1 teaspoon vanilla extract
1 tablespoon coconut extract
1 bag (7 ounces) sweetened flaked
    coconut (about 2½ cups)

 *A Note from Miss Kay*

This is a must for Easter lunch! Don't know why, it just is. I've seen it with the coconut dyed green, sprinkled on the top of the cake and topped with jelly beans. Too cute!

1. For the cake: Grease and flour two 8-inch cake pans. Prepare the mix according to package directions, adding the vanilla and coconut extracts to the batter. Bake as directed. Cool the layers to room temperature and then split them in half horizontally with a large serrated knife to make a total of 4 layers.

2. For the filling: In a large bowl, stir together the sugar, sour cream, and coconut. Place one cake layer on a cake plate or pedestal. Cover with one-third of the filling. Repeat twice more, ending with a cake layer that is bare on top.

3. For the frosting: In a large bowl, with an electric mixer on high speed, beat the butter until smooth and light, about 3 minutes. Add 4 cups of the powdered sugar, 1 cup at a time, beating until smooth after each addition. Quickly beat in the vanilla and coconut extracts. The frosting will be soft. Cover the top and sides of the cake with a thin, even layer of the frosting. This thin layer is called a crumb coat and helps prevent cake crumbs from mixing into the final layer of frosting.

4. Beat in enough of the remaining 1 to 2 cups powdered sugar to make a stiff frosting. Spread over the top and sides of the cake. Sprinkle the coconut over the top and sides of the cake, pressing lightly to help it adhere. Let sit at room temperature until the frosting sets up a bit.

5. Place the cake in an airtight carrier or cover with foil, taking care to not dislodge the coconut. Refrigerate at least 2 days, preferably 4 days, before serving.

Mamaw Jo's Chess Pie

■ *Makes 8 servings*

1 refrigerated piecrust (I use Pillsbury) or homemade (see Tip)

2 cups sugar

4 large eggs

2 tablespoons cornmeal

1 tablespoon all-purpose flour

¼ teaspoon salt

¼ cup whole milk

1 tablespoons distilled white vinegar

1 stick (¼ pound) butter, melted and slightly cooled

Lightly sweetened whipped cream, for serving

1. Bake the piecrust in a 9-inch pie plate according to package directions. (If using a homemade crust, see Tip.) Let cool on a wire rack for 15 minutes.

2. In a large bowl, whisk together the sugar and eggs until well blended. Whisk in the cornmeal, flour, salt, milk, and vinegar. Whisk in the melted butter.

3. Pour the mixture into the pie shell. Bake until the tip of a sharp knife inserted into the center comes out clean, 45 to 55 minutes. Shield the edge of the crust with foil if it browns too quickly. Cool the pie to room temperature on a wire rack.

4. Serve topped with a dollop of whipped cream.

Tip: If using a homemade crust, preheat the oven to 350°F. You can use the recipe on p. 118, but roll the crust out round instead of rectangular. Fit the pastry into a 9-inch pie plate. Line the pie shell with a sheet of foil or parchment paper, letting it extend past the rim by 2 inches. Fill with pie weights. Bake on a rack in lower third of the oven until the crust is set, about 15 minutes. Carefully lift out the foil and weights. Continue baking until the crust is pale golden, about 10 minutes more. Let cool on a rack.

 *A Note from Miss Kay*

This recipe is one of Chrys's mom's. Everyone calls her Mamaw Jo and she's a terrific cook. She says that filling an empty pie shell with pie weights keeps it from bubbling and bursting while it bakes. You can buy ceramic pie weights or a metal pie chain at kitchen supply stores, but it's fine to use uncooked dried beans or rice. Just don't eat the beans or rice and save them to use multiple times.

Sadie shares her basket with a little friend.

Everyone loves our Easter celebration!

- 5 -

Mother's Day

Celebrated on the Second Sunday in May

. . . . .

I stand fearlessly for small dogs, the American Flag,

motherhood and the Bible. That's why people love me.

—ART LINKLETTER

She speaks with wisdom,

and faithful instruction is on her tongue.

She watches over the affairs of her household

and does not eat the bread of idleness.

—PROVERBS 31:26–27 NIV

Recipes to Show Our Mothers We Care

Mother's Day

Celebrating Our Mothers

Sometimes I'm amazed that I'm the mother of four boys. Even with all the ups and downs we've gone through, I wouldn't trade any of it for anything. Because of Duck Commander, we've always worked together, but now with the TV show, we're together even more. And I couldn't be happier! My boys keep me laughing and make my heart happy.

Since my parents owned the local grocery store, my mom was a working mom. It was unusual at the time for a woman to work, but I didn't know it. It was just what we did. Women have always been hard workers. Even when they were stay-at-home moms, women a hundred years ago were busy tending to the cooking and laundry and cleaning. Those chores took many hours of each day, so mom wasn't always on the floor playing with her children. She was tending to tasks.

Great-grandaughters Bailey and Carly love frosting the best!

My mom and dad both worked in the store and that left me in the care of my grandmother. I didn't mind it at all. I loved my grandmother and learned many great lessons from her. She taught me how to cook and care for others, and she was a great role model. Looking back, I know my mom knew I was in the best hands possible with Nannie.

Being a mom is a lifetime honor and commitment, and Mother's Day is that day set aside to celebrate the mothers in our lives. On this special day, we may be celebrating

Jase (holding Reed), Granny, Alan, and Willie.

more than just one "mom," because being a mother isn't only defined as the one who gave birth to a child. Being a mother is about being the one who cares for and loves any child.

Most people are aware that Korie has five children, two of whom she didn't give birth to. Will was five weeks old when she adopted him, and Rebecca joined their family as an exchange student when she was sixteen. Not giving birth to these two doesn't change Korie's love and commitment to them. She adores them just as she does John Luke, Sadie, and Bella.

I have loved watching all of my daughters-in-law as they have grown in their roles as mothers. No two are exactly alike, but all are great moms. They love their children and seek ways to encourage and motivate them in the areas that each child needs.

Missy has navigated the rough road of having a child with a serious health issue. She bravely takes Mia to doctor's appointments and surgeries and still keeps up with all that her boys, Reed and Cole, have going on. Jessica has four children, each two years apart. Her days are very busy, but she manages her home with an unbelievable amount of energy. Her children, Lilly, Merritt, Priscilla, and River, are well behaved and a pleasure to be around because of Jessica's commitment to raise them that way. Lisa, Alan's wife, was the first of my daughters-in-law. She's raised her two girls, Alex and Anna, and is now a grandmother herself—giving me my first great-grandchildren. You can read about her story in the book she wrote with Al—*A New Season*. She's a mom who struggled with her faith when her girls were younger, but came back to be the strong leader they needed her to be. I love the women who are married to my sons and thank God every day for putting them in my life.

Mothers are the heart of a family and usually set the tone for the atmosphere of the home. Mother's Day is the day to say "thank you" and to let your mom (or moms!) know she is valued, appreciated, and loved. Instead of her cooking for you today, you cook for her! Then sit down together and enjoy the day!

French Toast Casserole

Cooking spray

8 large eggs

3 cups whole milk

2 teaspoons vanilla extract

¾ teaspoon salt

1 small loaf challah, brioche, or other rich bread (about 12 ounces), cut into 1-inch cubes

8 ounces honey-nut cream cheese

3 tablespoons butter, cut into small cubes

3 tablespoons sugar

1 teaspoon ground cinnamon

Warm maple syrup, for serving

1. Mist a 9 x 13-inch baking dish with cooking spray. In a large bowl, whisk together the eggs, milk, vanilla, and salt. Add the bread cubes and mix well. Pour into the baking dish.

2. Tuck rounded teaspoons of the cream cheese into the bread mixture, spacing them evenly. Cover and refrigerate overnight. Remove from the refrigerator 30 minutes before baking.

3. Preheat the oven to 350°F.

4. Dot the bread mixture with the butter. In a small bowl, stir together the sugar and cinnamon and sprinkle over the top.

5. Bake until a knife inserted into the center comes out clean, about 45 minutes. Let sit for 15 minutes before serving with the warm syrup.

 *A Note from Miss Kay*

French toast is so good, but it's time consuming and not everyone can be served at the same time. With this recipe, you still have the French toast taste, but it's easy to make and serve.

Candied Bacon

■ *Makes 8 servings*

Cooking spray
¾ cup packed light brown sugar
1 teaspoon ground cinnamon
Pinch of cayenne
Pinch of black pepper
1 pound thin-sliced bacon

1. Preheat the oven to 350°F. Line a rimmed baking sheet with foil. Place a wire rack inside the baking sheet. Generously mist the rack with cooking spray.

2. In a shallow container or pan, whisk together the brown sugar, cinnamon, cayenne, and black pepper. Coat both sides of the bacon slices in the sugar mixture, pressing to help it adhere.

3. Arrange the coated slices in a single layer on the wire rack. Sprinkle any remaining sugar mixture on top of the slices, trying to not let it spill onto the foil where it might burn.

4. Bake until the bacon is firm and the sugar mixture melts and darkens along the edges, about 45 minutes. Use a metal spatula to immediately lift the bacon off the rack and onto a serving platter. Let the bacon cool to room temperature. The bacon will continue to firm as it cools.

 *A Note from Miss Kay*

Can bacon be any tastier? Yes, it can! Add sugar to it. The perfect side to any brunch, this bacon recipe will make everyone happy, happy, happy!

Broccoli Cornbread

■ *Makes 8 servings*

Cooking spray

2 pouches (8.5 ounces each) cornbread mix, such as Martha White Buttermilk Cornbread

½ cup whole milk

1 cup cottage cheese

4 large eggs

2 teaspoons salt

½ cup very finely chopped onion

1 package (10 ounces) frozen chopped broccoli, thawed

1 stick (¼ pound) butter, melted

1¼ cups (5 ounces) grated cheddar cheese, divided

1. Preheat the oven to 375°F. Mist a 7 x 11-inch baking dish with cooking spray.

2. Pour the cornbread mix into a large bowl. In another large bowl, whisk together the milk, cottage cheese, eggs, and salt. Pour the egg mixture into the cornbread mix and stir to blend. Stir in the onion, broccoli, melted butter, and 1 cup of the cheese.

3. Scrape the batter into the baking dish. Sprinkle the remaining ¼ cup cheese over the top. Bake until golden brown and a wooden pick inserted into the center comes out clean, about 30 minutes. Serve warm.

 *A Note from Miss Kay*

This is as much a great side dish as it is a type of cornbread. It's very moist and might require a fork.

Cheese Grits

Makes 6 servings

2 cups water

2 cups whole milk

2 teaspoons salt, plus more to taste

1 cup quick-cooking grits (not instant)

1 cup (4 ounces) grated sharp cheddar cheese

½ stick (4 tablespoons) butter

1 teaspoon garlic powder

1 teaspoon onion powder

1 teaspoon hot sauce, or to taste

Black pepper

1. Bring the water, milk, and salt to a boil in a large saucepan. Whisking constantly, gradually add the grits. Reduce the heat and simmer, stirring occasionally, until the grits are thick, about 15 minutes. Stir more often as the grits begin to thicken.

2. Remove from the heat and add the cheese, butter, garlic powder, onion powder, hot sauce, and pepper to taste, stirring until smooth. Check the seasoning and serve hot.

 *A Note from Miss Kay*

Grits are definitely a Southern thing! Most folks love them just plain, but when you add garlic and cheese, you have a winner side dish. This can be served at any meal of the day!

Fresh Berry, Yogurt & Granola Parfaits

Makes 6 servings

4 cups vanilla yogurt

2 tablespoons honey

½ teaspoon ground ginger

2 cups granola

2 cups fresh berries, such as strawberries, blueberries, and/or blackberries

1. In a medium bowl, whisk together the yogurt, honey, and ginger.

2. Divide half of the yogurt mixture among 6 parfait or wine glasses. Top with half the granola and then half the berries. Repeat the layers.

3. Serve soon, while the granola is still crunchy.

A special day with my girls!

 *A Note from Miss Kay*

Mother's Day is such a special holiday and is celebrated many different ways. This parfait is good for brunches or dessert.

Hot Chicken Salad

Makes 8 to 12 servings

Cooking spray

7 tablespoons butter

1 cup chopped onion

1 cup chopped celery

1 can (10.75 ounces) cream of chicken
soup

½ cup mayonnaise

1 teaspoon salt

½ teaspoon black pepper

3 to 4 cups shredded cooked chicken
(see Note)

1 jar (4 ounces) diced pimento,
drained

1 cup slivered almonds

1 cup (4 ounces) grated sharp cheddar
cheese

1½ cups crushed buttery crackers,
such as Ritz

1. Preheat the oven to 350°F. Mist a 9 x 13-inch
baking dish with cooking spray.

2. Melt 4 tablespoons of the butter in a large skillet
over medium-high heat. Add the onion and celery
and cook, stirring often, until tender, about
5 minutes. Pour into a large bowl.

3. Stir the soup, mayonnaise, salt, and pepper
into the cooked vegetables. Stir in the chicken,
pimento, almonds, and cheese. Scrape into the
baking dish.

4. In a small saucepan, melt the remaining 3 tablespoons butter. Toss the cracker crumbs with
the melted butter and sprinkle over the chicken
mixture.

5. Bake until golden brown and bubbling, about
30 minutes.

 *A Note from Miss Kay*

*Not everyone loves pimentos, so feel free to leave them out if you want to. A plain rotisserie chicken is
a great way to get cooked chicken to use in recipes. One chicken yields about 3½ cups of meat.*

Stuffed Tomatoes

■ *Makes 8 servings*

8 medium tomatoes

2 teaspoons salt

½ stick (4 tablespoons) butter, divided

1 cup finely chopped onion

4 garlic cloves, finely chopped

2 teaspoons Italian seasoning

3 cups coarse, fresh bread crumbs

1 cup grated Asiago or Parmesan cheese, divided

2 tablespoons finely chopped flat-leaf parsley

1 large egg, lightly beaten

Black pepper

1. Preheat the oven to 375°F.

2. Use a serrated knife to cut the tops off the tomatoes, taking off just enough to reveal the flesh. Use a sharp spoon or melon baller to scoop out the tomato flesh and seeds. Leave the walls of the tomato shells intact. Generously season the inside of the tomato shells with the salt and turn them upside down on paper towels to drain for 15 minutes.

3. Meanwhile, heat 2 tablespoons of the butter in a large skillet over medium-high heat. Add the onion and cook, stirring occasionally, until tender, about 5 minutes. Stir in the garlic and Italian seasoning and cook 1 minute more. Scrape into a large bowl.

4. Heat the remaining 2 tablespoons of butter in the skillet. Add the bread crumbs and cook, stirring often, until golden, about 3 minutes. Add to the bowl with the onions. Stir in ¾ cup of the Asiago, the parsley, and egg. Season with pepper to taste.

5. Arrange the tomatoes in a baking dish just large enough to hold them upright. Spoon the filling into the tomatoes. Sprinkle with the remaining ¼ cup Asiago.

6. Bake until the topping is browned and the stuffing is heated through, about 30 minutes.

 *A Note from Miss Kay*

You might not be a tomato eater until you taste this one. So delicious!

Fruit Juice Spritzers

Makes 6 to 8 servings

4 cups orange-mango juice, chilled

4 cups ginger ale or orange-flavored sparkling water, chilled

Maraschino cherries and orange slices, for garnish

Mint leaves, for garnish

In a large pitcher, stir together the juice and the ginger ale. Refrigerate until chilled before serving. Garnish with the mint, cherries, and orange slices.

Korie enjoys Mother's Day with her mom, Chrys, and three daughters.

 *A Note from Miss Kay*

This is a recipe even your kids can do to make mom a special treat. It's the perfect drink for a Mother's Day brunch.

Berries & Cream Angel Food Cake

Makes 6 to 8 servings

1 (8-inch) angel food cake

1 pint fresh blackberries or other berries, divided

1 container (12 ounces) frozen whipped topping, such as Cool Whip, thawed and divided

1. Turn the cake upside down. Use a serrated knife to cut off the bottom crust in one large slice that is about ¾ inch thick. Short strokes with a sawing motion work best. Use your fingers to gently pull out the fluffy interior of the cake, leaving a ¾-inch shell. (You won't need the part you pull out for this recipe, so you can eat it or use it for something else.)

2. In a medium bowl, fold half of the berries into 1 cup of the whipped topping. Spoon into the cake. Replace the bottom crust and press gently to close the cake. Carefully turn the cake top-side up and place it on a cake plate or platter. The replaced slice is now on the bottom.

3. Frost the cake with the remaining whipped topping. Garnish with the remaining berries. Place in a cake carrier or cover loosely with plastic wrap and refrigerate until chilled before serving, at least 2 hours. If you are in a hurry, place the cake in the freezer for about 15 minutes. Serve chilled.

 *A Note from Miss Kay*

If you are buying the cake, be sure to notice its size. Some are about 8 inches wide (6 to 8 servings) and others around 10 to 12 inches wide (10 to 16 servings). This recipe uses a small cake, so you'll need to double the other ingredients if you buy a big cake.

Little Lemon Ice Box Pies with Mile-High Meringue

Makes 8 servings

8 (3-inch) mini graham cracker crust shells

4 large egg yolks

1 can (14 ounces) sweetened condensed milk, such as Eagle Brand

Grated zest of 1 lemon (about 1 tablespoon)

½ cup fresh lemon juice

6 large egg whites

½ teaspoon cream of tartar

½ teaspoon vanilla extract

¾ cup sugar

1. Preheat the oven to 350°F. Arrange the pie shells on a rimmed baking sheet.

2. In a large bowl, whisk together the egg yolks and sweetened condensed milk until smooth. Whisk in the lemon zest and lemon juice until smooth. Divide filling among the pie shells. Bake for 15 minutes.

3. Meanwhile, make the meringue. In another large bowl, with an electric mixer on low speed, beat the egg whites, cream of tartar, and vanilla until cloudy. Increase the speed to high and beat until soft peaks form. With the mixer running, gradually add the sugar and beat until stiff peaks form.

4. Top the warm pies with the meringue. Use the back of a spoon to create pretty swirls. Return the pies to the oven and bake until the meringue is golden, about 20 minutes. Transfer the pies to a wire cooling rack to cool to room temperature, then refrigerate until chilled, about 4 hours.

 *A Note from Miss Kay*

Instead of individual pies, you can bake the filling in a standard 9-inch graham cracker crust. Either way, it's the best!

- 6 -

Father's Day

Celebrated on the Third Sunday in June

. . . . .

My mom and dad gave their kids the greatest gift of all—

the gift of unconditional love.

They cared deeply about who we would be,

and much less about what we would do.

—MITT ROMNEY

Fathers, do not exasperate your children;

instead, bring them up in the training

and instruction of the Lord.

—EPHESIANS 6:4 NIV

Recipes for the Men in My Life

The Guys

Celebrating Fathers

I lost my father when I was fourteen. I've lived many years now without him and often wonder how my life would have been different if he had lived longer. My memories of him stop as I entered my teen years, but I remember him as the protector of the family and someone I loved very much. He took me hunting and fishing, so my love for these outdoor activities grew during this time, but mostly I loved just being with my dad. I know that's why I was attracted to Phil. He was like my daddy in my fourteen-year-old eyes. My daddy wasn't perfect—I knew that about him too. But he took care of our family, and I respected him. He wasn't a church-going man, but he loved for me to sing "The Old Rugged Cross" and "What a Friend We Have in Jesus" to him. Maybe it's because he died when I was young that those memories are very fresh in my mind. I didn't have the opportunity to make new memories, so I cherish the old ones.

I'm saddened today when I see the lack of respect given to our dads in America. So many television shows and

I love beach time with my boys. Jep and his family stayed home this year because Jessica was pregnant with one of our sweet grandbabies.

movies portray the dad of the family as incompetent instead of the strong man God has called them to be. Even sadder, men are responding to these portrayals and are not living with the boldness of purpose they were designed to have. I'm so blessed to see all of my sons as dads. No two of them have the same "dad personality." Alan's two daughters are now grown, but he was the loving leader in his family when they were growing up, and he now enjoys his three granddaughters and one grandson. He still helps lead his growing family. Jase is a very hands-on dad. He loves to coach their Little League teams and get in the yard and throw a football. He is a strong spiritual leader and has studied the Bible with many of his boy's friends. Willie is more about leading through work than play. He used to be the director at a summer camp, and he and John Luke spent many hours together repairing and building things. Willie also takes his sense of humor into his parenting, and his kids love to laugh with him, not at him. Jep, the newest dad, helps Jessica in every area. With four children, there's always something to do, and Jep partners with Jessica in raising their kids. All of them are the leaders of their families that Phil and I dreamed they would be, and we're very proud of them. I'm proud that they are not believing the lies of the world and that they know God has created them to lead their families. They take that job very seriously.

This month is about celebrating a holiday named "Father's Day," but dads deserve to feel honored and loved every day. If your dad is still living, take time to let him know how much you love and appreciate him. And let your husband know what an amazing job he is doing as the leader of your family. Enjoy the moments. Celebrate with your dad!

Mini Sausages in Grape Jelly Barbecue Sauce

Makes 12 to 16 servings

1 bottle (12 or 14 ounces) barbecue sauce

1 jar (12 ounces) grape jelly

2 pounds smoked cocktail sausage links, such as Hillshire Farms Lit'l Smokies, drained

1. Stir together the barbecue sauce and jelly in a large saucepan. Cook over medium heat, stirring, to melt the jelly.

2. Add the sausages and stir to coat. Cook until the sausages are warmed through, about 5 minutes. Serve warm.

Here's Willie as a proud father to beautiful Sadie at homecoming.

A Note from Miss Kay

This is a favorite of all the Robertson men. You can also prepare this recipe in a slow cooker. Just stir together the ingredients in the cooker and cook on the high setting for 2 hours. Stir well before serving. Reduce the setting to low to keep them warm.

Fried Pickles

Makes 8 to 10 servings

1 cup buttermilk

1 tablespoon hot sauce

1 jar (16 ounces) dill pickle slices, drained

1 cup cornmeal

1 cup all-purpose flour

1½ tablespoons seasoned salt, such as Lawry's, plus more to taste

½ teaspoon paprika

½ teaspoon black pepper

¼ teaspoon cayenne, or to taste

Peanut oil, for deep-frying

Ranch dressing, for dipping

1. In a large bowl, whisk together the buttermilk and hot sauce. Add the pickle slices and stir to coat.

2. In a shallow dish, whisk together the cornmeal, flour, seasoned salt, paprika, pepper, and cayenne.

3. Pour the oil to a depth of 2 inches in a large, deep cast-iron skillet or deep-fryer. Heat the oil to 365°F on a deep-fry thermometer.

4. Working with about ¼ cup of pickles at a time, remove them from the buttermilk mixture, let excess drip off, and coat lightly and evenly in the cornmeal mixture.

5. Slip coated pickles one at a time into the hot oil, making sure not to fry too many at once; they should be able to float freely. Fry the pickles until the coating is dark golden brown, 3 to 5 minutes. Remove with a slotted spoon to drain on paper towels. Sprinkle the hot pickles with a little more seasoned salt, if desired. Repeat until all the pickles are fried. Between batches, discard any large clumps that might form in the cornmeal mixture and be sure to let the oil return to 365°F.

6. Serve hot with ranch dressing for dipping.

 *A Note from Miss Kay*

Even non-pickle lovers seem to like fried pickles. This recipe is a favorite at Willie's diner in our hometown of West Monroe. Serve them with anything!

Mashed Potato Casserole

Makes 8 servings

3 pounds russet (baking) potatoes, peeled and cut into 2-inch chunks

1 tablespoon salt

6 garlic cloves

Cooking spray

1 package (8 ounces) cream cheese, at room temperature

1 cup sour cream

½ cup whole milk, warmed

½ stick (4 tablespoons) butter, at room temperature

1 teaspoon seasoned salt, such as Lawry's

Black pepper

¼ cup panko bread crumbs

¼ cup finely grated Parmesan cheese

¼ teaspoon paprika

1 tablespoon butter, melted

1. Place the potatoes in large pot and cover with cold water. Add the salt and garlic. Bring to a boil over high heat, reduce the heat, partially cover, and simmer until the potatoes are tender when pierced with a knife, about 20 minutes. Drain well and pour into a large bowl. Mash the potatoes and garlic with a hand-held potato masher.

2. Preheat the oven to 350°F. Mist a shallow 2-quart baking dish with cooking spray.

3. Add the cream cheese, sour cream, milk, and butter to the potatoes and stir until smooth. Stir in the seasoned salt and pepper to taste. Scrape into the baking dish and smooth the top.

4. In a small bowl, stir together the panko, Parmesan, and paprika. Drizzle with the melted butter and toss to coat. Sprinkle over the potato mixture.

5. Bake until the potatoes are heated through and the topping is golden brown, about 30 minutes.

 *A Note from Miss Kay*

This recipe takes mashed potatoes to another level! The whole family will love this recipe. Serve it with those great pork chops (see page 111) or chicken-fried steaks (see page 115), and you'll be the party favorite.

Smothered Pork Chops

Makes 4 servings

4 large bone-in pork chops, about 1 inch thick

1 teaspoon salt

½ teaspoon black pepper

1 teaspoon Creole seasoning blend, such as Tony Chachere's

2 tablespoons vegetable oil

2 tablespoons butter

1 large onion, halved and thinly sliced (about 3 cups)

¼ cup all-purpose flour

1½ cups chicken broth, warmed

½ cup buttermilk

1. Season both sides of the chops with the salt, pepper, and Creole seasoning.

2. In a large cast-iron skillet, heat the oil and butter over medium-high heat. Add the chops and let cook undisturbed until seared and browned on the bottom, about 3 minutes. Turn with tongs and brown the other side, about 3 minutes more. Transfer to a plate and tent loosely with foil.

3. Add the onion to the skillet. Stir to loosen the browned bits from the bottom of the skillet. Cook, stirring often, until golden and tender, about 15 minutes. Reduce the heat and add a splash of the broth if the onions begin to scorch.

4. Sprinkle the flour over the onions and stir to coat. Cook, stirring, for 2 minutes. Add the broth in a slow, steady stream and stir until incorporated. Cook, stirring slowly and constantly, until the gravy begins to thicken. Stir in the buttermilk. The mixture might look curdled at first but will incorporate as you stir. Reduce the heat and simmer until the gravy is thick.

5. Return the pork chops and any accumulated juices to the skillet. Gently push the chops down into the gravy and simmer until cooked through, about 10 minutes. Check the seasoning. Serve warm.

 *A Note from Miss Kay*

I admit I don't make pork chops as often as I used to, but I always wonder why I don't when I do! (Did that make sense?)

Shrimp & Andouille Gumbo

■ *Makes 6 to 8 servings*

2 pounds shell-on medium (26/30 count) fresh shrimp

4 cups chicken broth

1 cup water

½ cup peanut oil

½ cup all-purpose flour

1 green bell pepper, chopped (about 1 cup)

1 medium onion, chopped (about 1½ cups)

3 celery stalks, chopped (about 1½ cups)

4 garlic cloves, chopped

1 tablespoon Cajun seasoning blend, such as Duck Commander or any brand

1 tablespoon Worcestershire sauce

12 ounces smoked andouille sausage, cut into ¼-inch rounds

1 pound fresh or thawed frozen okra, cut into ½-inch rounds

Salt, black pepper, and cayenne

8 cups hot freshly cooked long-grain white rice

1 bunch green onions (scallions), thinly sliced

A few sprigs of flat-leaf parsley, for garnish (optional)

Hot sauce, for serving

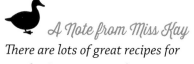

A Note from Miss Kay

There are lots of great recipes for gumbo floating around Louisiana. Try this one. You will love it!

1. Peel the shrimp and reserve the shells. Devein the shrimp, put in a medium bowl, cover, and refrigerate until needed. Rinse the shells and place in a large saucepan. Add the broth and water. Bring to a boil, reduce the heat, and simmer 30 minutes. Strain into a large bowl, pressing firmly on the solids to extract all the stock before discarding the solids. Rinse the saucepan. Return the stock to the pan, and keep warm over very low heat.

2. Heat the oil in a large, heavy pot or Dutch oven over medium heat for 2 minutes. Sprinkle the flour over the hot oil and whisk until smooth. Cook, stirring constantly with a wooden spatula or spoon, until the roux is the color of peanut butter, about 15 minutes. Reduce the heat to low and continue cooking and stirring until the roux is the color of milk chocolate, 10 to 15 minutes more.

3. Stir the bell pepper, onion, and celery into the roux. Cook, stirring often, until tender, about 5 minutes. Add the garlic and Cajun seasoning and cook 1 minute.

4. Whisking constantly, add the warm shrimp stock in a slow, steady stream, whisking until the roux is smooth. Stir in the Worcestershire sauce and simmer for 30 minutes.

5. Stir in the sausage and okra and simmer until the okra is tender, about 10 minutes. Season with the salt, pepper, and cayenne to taste.

6. Stir in the shrimp. Simmer only until the shrimp are opaque, about 5 minutes.

7. Serve hot over the rice, topped with green onions and a sprig of parsley. Pass a bottle of hot sauce at the table.

Quick Three-Seed Pan Rolls

■ *Makes 1 dozen*

1 teaspoon dill seeds

1 teaspoon poppy seeds

1 teaspoon sesame seeds

½ teaspoon coarse salt

12 frozen unbaked rolls, such as
  Rhodes

1 egg white, beaten

Cooking spray

3 tablespoons butter, melted

1. In a small bowl, stir together the dill seeds, poppy seeds, sesame seeds, and salt.

2. Dip the top of each frozen roll in the egg white and then dip into the seeds. Arrange the rolls, seeded-side up, in a lightly greased 9-inch round cake pan. Mist a sheet of plastic wrap with cooking spray and place loosely over the pan. Let rise in a warm place (around 85°F) that is free from drafts until the rolls double in size, 3 to 4 hours.

3. Preheat the oven to 350°F. Uncover the rolls and bake until golden brown, about 20 minutes. Drizzle the tops with the melted butter and serve warm.

I love seeing my sons be awesome dads.

A Note from Miss Kay

This is one of those "almost homemade" recipes. Remember that different brands of rolls might have different instructions for rising and baking. Be sure to read the package.

Chicken-Fried Steak with Milk Gravy

Makes 8 servings

1 cup all-purpose flour
1 teaspoon baking powder
1 teaspoon salt
½ teaspoon black pepper
1 teaspoon garlic powder
¾ cup buttermilk
1 large egg
1 teaspoon hot sauce
8 cube steaks (6 ounces each)
Peanut oil or canola oil, for pan-frying
2 cups milk, warmed

1. In a shallow bowl, whisk together the flour, baking powder, salt, pepper, and garlic powder. In a second shallow bowl, whisk together the buttermilk, egg, and hot sauce.

2. Coat the steaks lightly and evenly in the flour mixture. Coat the steaks in the egg mixture, letting any excess drip off. Coat the steaks again in the flour mixture. Set aside in a single layer. Reserve a ¼ cup of the flour mixture to use in the gravy and discard the rest.

3. Pour the oil to a depth of 1 inch into a large cast-iron skillet. Heat over high heat until the oil shimmers. Working in batches, lower the steaks into the hot oil and fry, turning once, until deep golden brown on both sides, about 3 minutes per side. Move the cooked steaks to a plate and tent loosely with foil to keep warm.

4. Pour off all but 4 tablespoons of the fat from the pan, leaving the browned bits on the bottom of the pan. Whisk in the reserved flour mixture and cook over medium heat for 2 minutes, whisking constantly. Whisk in the warm milk and cook, stirring slowly and constantly with a spatula, until the gravy comes to a boil and thickens. Check the seasoning.

5. Serve the steaks with the gravy.

 *A Note from Miss Kay*

Seriously, what man doesn't like chicken-fried steak? All of mine do! Making gravy scares new cooks, but it's really easy. Just follow the recipe.

Coca-Cola Cake

Makes 16 servings

Cake

2 sticks (½ pound) butter, at room temperature
⅓ cup unsweetened cocoa powder
1 cup Coca-Cola (not diet)
2 cups all-purpose flour
1⅓ cups sugar
1 teaspoon baking soda
2 large eggs, at room temperature
½ cup buttermilk
1 teaspoon vanilla extract
1½ cups miniature marshmallows

Frosting

1 stick (¼ pound) butter
¼ cup unsweetened cocoa powder
⅓ cup Coca-Cola
3 cups powdered sugar, sifted
½ teaspoon vanilla extract
1 cup chopped pecans

1. For the cake: Preheat the oven to 350°F. Grease and flour a 9 x 13-inch baking pan.

2. In a small saucepan, combine the butter, cocoa powder, and Coca-Cola and cook over medium heat, stirring, until the butter melts. Remove from the heat.

3. In a large bowl, whisk together the flour, sugar, and baking soda. Add the butter mixture and whisk until smooth. Whisk in the eggs. Whisk in the buttermilk and vanilla. Fold in the marshmallows with a rubber spatula.

4. Scrape the batter into the baking pan. Bake until a wooden pick inserted into the center comes out clean, 25 to 30 minutes. Make the frosting during last 10 minutes of baking time so that it is ready to pour over the warm cake.

5. For the frosting: In a large saucepan, stir together the butter, cocoa powder, and Coca-Cola. Cook over medium heat, stirring until the butter melts. Remove from the heat and whisk in the powdered sugar and vanilla until smooth. Stir in the pecans.

6. Pour the warm frosting over the warm cake and spread evenly. Let cool to room temperature.

 *A Note from Miss Kay*

Everyone knows I love Coke Zero, but don't use it for this recipe! Don't tell your family what's in the cake and see if they can taste the Coca-Cola.

Peach Cobbler

■ *Makes 12 servings*

Crust

3 cups all-purpose flour

1 teaspoon salt

1 cup butter-flavored shortening, such as Crisco, chilled

1 large egg

2 tablespoons distilled white vinegar

1 to 3 tablespoons ice water, as needed

Filling

2½ cups sugar

¾ cup all-purpose flour

½ teaspoon salt

½ teaspoon ground cinnamon

4 cups fresh peeled and sliced or thawed frozen sliced peaches

Vanilla ice cream, for serving (optional)

A Note from Miss Kay

This cobbler will work with any fruit. We love peaches, but cherries or apples are great too.

1. For the crust: In a large bowl, whisk together the flour and salt. Work in the shortening with a pastry blender or your fingertips until the mixture is crumbly with a few pieces of shortening the size of small green peas.

2. In a small bowl, whisk together the egg, vinegar, and 1 tablespoon ice water. Drizzle over the flour mixture and stir with a fork to form large clumps of dough that pull in all the dry ingredients. Add more water 1 teaspoon at a time if the mixture is too dry.

3. Pour the clumps onto a lightly floured surface and knead gently to form a ball. Divide the ball in half. Flatten each half into a disk. Wrap each disk tightly in plastic wrap and refrigerate for at least 1 hour and up to overnight.

4. Preheat the oven to 375°F.

5. Place one disk of dough on a lightly floured surface and roll into a rectangle about 9 x 13 inches. Fit the dough into the bottom of 9 x 13-inch baking pan, pressing it into place with your fingers. Press together any holes or tears. Bake until golden brown, about 10 minutes. Leave the oven on.

6. Meanwhile, roll the second disk of dough into a rectangle that is about 9 x 13 inches. Leave this piece whole or cut it into strips with a pizza cutter or sharp knife.

7. For the filling: In a large bowl, whisk together the sugar, flour, salt, and cinnamon. Add the peaches and toss to coat.

8. Spread the peaches over the bottom crust. Place the top crust over the peaches. If the crust is

whole, cut a few steam vents in the top with the tip of a sharp knife.

9. Bake until the crust is golden brown and the filling bubbles, about 45 minutes. Cool 15 minutes before serving warm. Top with a scoop of ice cream, if you wish.

Pineapple Upside-Down Cake

Makes 8 servings

½ stick (4 tablespoons) butter
1 cup packed light brown sugar
1 can (20 ounces) juice-packed pineapple rings
12 maraschino cherries without stems, drained
1 box yellow cake mix
Ingredients listed on cake mix package for preparing batter

1. Preheat the oven to 325°F. In a 10-inch cast-iron skillet, melt the butter over medium-high heat. Add the brown sugar and stir until melted.

2. Reserving the juice, drain the pineapple. Arrange the pineapple rings over the sugar mixture. You might have a few rings leftover. Place a cherry in the center of each ring, plus a few around the edge of the pan.

3. Prepare the cake batter according to package directions, but replace the water with an equal amount of the reserved pineapple juice. Scrape the batter into the skillet.

4. Bake until a wooden pick inserted into center of the cake comes out clean, 40 to 45 minutes. As soon as the cake comes out of the oven, run a thin knife around the edge. Cover the skillet with a large serving plate. Using oven mitts, hold the skillet and plate firmly together and quickly flip the whole thing over. Let sit for 5 minutes and then lift the skillet straight up. The cake should fall easily onto the plate, but if any of the fruit sticks to the pan, gently pry it loose and replace it on the cake. Cool at least 30 minutes before serving warm or at room temperature.

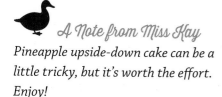

A Note from Miss Kay

Pineapple upside-down cake can be a little tricky, but it's worth the effort. Enjoy!

Si with Miss Kay and Mia

Independence Day

Celebrated on the Fourth Day of July

· · · · ·

Freedom is never more than one generation away from extinction.

We didn't pass it to our children in the bloodstream.

It must be fought for, protected,

and handed on for them to do the same.

—RONALD REAGAN

The Lord is the Spirit.

Where the Spirit of the Lord is,

there is freedom.

—2 CORINTHIANS 3:17 NIV

Recipes to Celebrate
Our Nation's Freedom

Sadie and John Luke dress up for the day.

Celebrating Our Freedom

Our family goes to the beach every summer. It's a time of renewal as we enjoy the summer sun and sand. Several summers ago we were there over the Fourth of July. I think the grandkids ranged from about two years old to maybe nine or ten at the time. They love to entertain us, and we are often called to the living room for a "performance." Well, that year they made a makeshift auditorium under the beach house we had rented. All the beach chairs were lined up in rows, and a flat area was left open for their stage. After many hours under the house, they presented us with invitations to the show. We had no idea what to expect, but we were in for a treat. Those little kids had put together a celebration for the Fourth of July like little professionals. They sang patriotic songs, quoted scripture, and recited the pledge. I'm pretty sure there wasn't a dry eye in the "outside house."

I love that our children are learning about patriotism. To me being patriotic just means to be a cheerleader for our country. I was a cheerleader for my school when I was a teenager. That meant I was loyal to my school and always ready to cheer them on to victory. It didn't mean I agreed with everything going on in the school. It just meant I valued my school and wanted to support it. Being a cheerleader for our country is the same. We will never agree on every issue, but we can agree to support and honor the heritage we have as Americans and to stand proud, knowing that many men and women have sacrificed for the freedom we sometimes take for granted.

Most of you are aware that Uncle Si served our country for many years. I'll never forget when he had to go overseas for the first time. It was during the Vietnam War, and we were nervous for his safety. I even named Jase (Jason Silas) after Uncle Si, to honor him for serving well. Phil was named after an uncle who lost his life in service during World War II, so it seemed appropriate to name one of our sons after Si. Si survived Vietnam and many other stations of duty in his nearly twenty-five years of serving our country. We were proud of his service and never took what he was doing lightly. All of Phil's other siblings chose college and careers, but Si never felt like college was for him. He was very smart, but college just didn't interest him. The military did, and he made it a career. Now Si and our entire family make it a point to honor those serving our country any way we can. In 2013, Willie and Jep were asked to be a part of the USO tour at Christmas and Sadie was asked to donate dresses from her prom line to daughters of military families for their proms. She was able to go to New York and actually help the girls pick their dresses. Our family was so blessed to help out at these events, and we look forward to many more opportunities.

Cheering on my team!

This month and all year long, celebrate the freedom we get to enjoy because of other's sacrifices. Raise a flag, hang a banner, recite the pledge, wear red, white, and blue, put on a play, cook hamburgers, hug a serviceman—whatever, just celebrate!

Black Bean & Corn Dip

Makes 12 servings

1 can (15 ounces) black beans, drained and rinsed

1 can (11 ounces) shoepeg corn, drained

1 can (15 ounces) petite diced tomatoes, drained

1 can (4 ounces) diced green chiles

½ cup finely diced onion

1 cup finely diced bell pepper

Juice of 1 lime

2 tablespoons extra-virgin olive oil

Garlic salt

1 tablespoon chopped cilantro, or to taste

Corn or tortilla chips, for serving

1. In a medium glass bowl, stir together the beans, corn, tomatoes, chiles, onion, bell pepper, lime juice, and oil. Season with the garlic salt to taste.

2. Cover and refrigerate until chilled, stirring occasionally. Stir in the cilantro just before serving with the chips.

 *A Note from Miss Kay*

The Fourth of July is great for large crowds and everyone comes hungry. This dip is perfect to have out when the crowds start arriving.

Marinated Tomatoes

Makes 6 servings

⅓ cup extra-virgin olive oil

¼ cup red wine vinegar

1 teaspoon salt

½ teaspoon sugar

1 garlic clove, very finely chopped

2 tablespoons grated or very finely chopped sweet onion, such as Vidalia

2 pounds ripe tomatoes, cored and cut into bite-size wedges or chunks

3 tablespoons finely chopped fresh basil

1. In a large shallow serving dish, whisk together the oil, vinegar, salt, sugar, garlic, and onion. Add the tomatoes and toss gently to coat.

2. Cover and refrigerate until chilled, at least 2 hours. Just before serving, stir in the basil.

 *A Note from Miss Kay*

This easy dish is perfect for a summer holiday when fresh tomatoes are easy to find. Plus, you can do this dish ahead of time.

Barbecue Baked Beans

Makes 8 servings

½ pound bacon, chopped

1 small onion, chopped (about 1 cup)

2 cans (28 ounces each) baked beans or pork-and-beans

2 tablespoons yellow mustard

2 tablespoons packed light brown sugar

¼ cup barbecue sauce

2 tablespoons apple cider vinegar

1. In a large skillet, cook the bacon over medium-high heat until beginning to crisp, about 10 minutes. Stir in the onion and cook, stirring often, until the bacon is crisp and the onions are tender, about 8 minutes more.

2. Stir in the beans, mustard, brown sugar, barbecue sauce, and vinegar.

3. Simmer over medium-low heat, stirring occasionally, until the liquid thickly coats the beans, about 20 minutes. Stir often as they thicken to keep them from scorching on the bottom. Serve warm.

The whole family on stage together. Does it get any better than this?

 *A Note from Miss Kay*

Any brand of baked beans will work, though I prefer Van Camp's.

Grilled Corn on the Cob

Makes 8 servings

8 ears freshly picked corn

1 stick (¼ pound) butter, at room temperature

2 teaspoons Montreal Steak seasoning

1 teaspoon freshly grated lime zest

1. Heat a gas grill to medium-high heat or heat coals in a charcoal grill until they glow bright orange and are covered in gray ash. Shuck the corn. You can pull the husks off completely or pull them back and tie them together with kitchen twine just under the cob to make a handle.

2. In a small bowl, stir together the butter, seasoning, and lime zest.

3. Arrange the ears around the edge of the grill grate so that the corn kernels are over the heat but the shucks (if attached) extend beyond the grate so that they are less likely to burn. Grill the corn, rotating to cook evenly on all sides, until the corn is just tender and some of the kernels are golden brown or lightly charred.

4. Spread the butter mixture over the hot corn and serve at once.

 *A Note from Miss Kay*

The key to good corn is to eat it as soon as possible after it's picked. Look for ears that look firm and feel full when gently squeezed. The silks should be pale and dry. Some people grill corn that hasn't been shucked, but we like that nice grilled flavor that comes from letting the ears cook directly on the grill grate so that some of the kernels get browned and lightly charred.

Inside-Out Cheeseburgers

■ *Makes 8 servings*

2 pounds ground beef (80% lean)
2 teaspoons Worcestershire sauce
2 teaspoons garlic powder
1 teaspoon salt
½ teaspoon black pepper
8 ounces Velveeta, sharp cheddar
   cheese, or blue cheese, cut into
   ½-inch cubes, at room temperature
8 hamburger buns
Your favorite burger toppings

1. In a large bowl, mix the beef, Worcestershire sauce, garlic powder, salt, and pepper. Form the meat into 8 patties of equal size, each about ½ inch thick. Press 2 cubes of cheese into the center of each patty, making sure that they are covered. Refrigerate while the grill heats.

2. Heat a gas grill to medium-high or heat coals in a charcoal grill until they glow bright orange and are covered in gray ash.

3. Grill the burgers until dark grill marks appear on the bottom, about 4 minutes. Flip the burgers. Cook until dark grill marks appear on the second side and the burgers are just cooked through, about 4 minutes more. Do not press the burgers with a spatula while cooking. Move the burgers to a clean plate, tent loosely with foil, and let rest 5 minutes.

4. Meanwhile, arrange the buns along the outer edge of the grill to lightly toast, if you wish.

5. Serve the burgers on buns with toppings of your choice.

 *A Note from Miss Kay*

We love cheese, lettuce, tomatoes, and dill pickles on our hamburgers. All the guys like mustard, but I like mayo. Phil insists on purple onions if we have onions.

Lemonade Chicken

■ *Makes 6 to 8 servings*

1 can (12 ounces) frozen lemonade
    concentrate, thawed

¼ cup soy sauce

2 teaspoons seasoned salt, such as
    Lawry's

1 teaspoon dried thyme

½ teaspoon black pepper

4 pounds bone-in chicken thighs or
    leg quarters, skin removed

1. Pour the lemonade concentrate, soy sauce, seasoned salt, thyme, and pepper into a large zip-top freezer bag. Add the chicken, squeeze out the excess air, and tightly seal the bag. Let sit at room temperature for 30 minutes. Don't let the chicken sit out any longer: it's not safe, plus leaving it in the lemon marinade for too long makes the chicken tough.

2. Meanwhile, heat a grill to medium-high heat. Drain and discard the marinade. Arrange the chicken pieces on a well-oiled grill grate, cover, and cook until the chicken shows grill marks on the bottom, about 10 minutes. Turn with tongs and grill the other side, about 10 minutes more. When done, an instant-read thermometer inserted into the thickest part of the thigh without touching bone registers 165°F. Serve warm.

 *A Note from Miss Kay*

Bone-in dark chicken meat is the easiest to grill because it stays moist and juicy. However, if your family prefers white meat, use bone-in split chicken breasts. Don't try this with boneless, skinless chicken breasts, especially if they've been frozen.

Creole Potato Salad

Makes 8 to 10 servings

2 pounds unpeeled new potatoes, scrubbed and halved or quartered

2 tablespoons Creole seasoning blend, such as Tony Chachere's

1 cup mayonnaise

2 tablespoons Creole mustard

2 tablespoons olive juice or dill pickle juice

¼ cup very finely chopped stuffed green olives

½ cup very finely chopped green bell pepper

½ cup very finely chopped celery

¼ cup very finely chopped green onions (scallions)

¼ cup finely chopped flat-leaf parsley

4 hard-cooked eggs, chopped (see Tip on page 75)

½ cup chopped crisp-cooked bacon (optional)

Salt, black pepper, and cayenne

Paprika, for garnish

1. Place the potatoes in a large saucepan and cover with cold water. Add the Creole seasoning. Bring to a boil, reduce the heat, and cook at a low boil until tender when pierced with tip of a sharp knife, about 20 minutes. Don't let them get waterlogged. Drain and let sit for 5 minutes. Pour into a large bowl.

2. Meanwhile, in a medium bowl, whisk together the mayonnaise, mustard, and olive juice.

3. Pour the mayonnaise mixture over the warm potatoes and stir to coat. Stir in the olives, bell pepper, celery, green onions, parsley, eggs, and bacon (if using). Season with salt, pepper, and cayenne to taste.

4. Cover and refrigerate until lightly chilled. Sprinkle with paprika just before serving.

 *A Note from Miss Kay*

Potato salad is a family favorite. I love the little extra spice in this Creole recipe. Great for a large group!

Paper Cup Strawberry Popsicles

Makes 8 servings

2 pounds very ripe fresh or thawed
    frozen strawberries, caps removed

¼ cup sugar

2 tablespoons lemon juice

2 tablespoons light corn syrup

Cooking spray

1. In a large bowl, crush the berries. Stir in the sugar and let sit until the berries release some juice, about 30 minutes. Pour into a blender, add the lemon juice and corn syrup, and puree.

2. Coat eight 6-ounce paper cups with cooking spray. Divide the strawberry mixture among the cups. Cover the top of each cup with a double thickness of foil. Make a small slit in the center of the foil with the tip of a paring knife. Insert a wooden popsicle stick into each slit, using the foil to hold it in place.

3. Freeze until firm, at least 4 hours and preferably overnight. Discard the foil. Snip the edge of the paper cups with scissors and then peel away the paper. Serve at once.

 *A Note from Miss Kay*

This is one of those recipes that the kids can help make. If you need more, just double everything.

Strawberry Pretzel Congealed Salad

■ *Makes 12 servings*

Crust

2 cups finely crushed pretzels
(6 ounces)

2 tablespoons sugar

¼ teaspoon ground cinnamon

1½ sticks (12 tablespoons) butter,
melted

Topping

1 package (8 ounces) cream cheese, at
room temperature

1 cup sugar

1 container (8 ounces) frozen
whipped topping, such as Cool
Whip, thawed

2 boxes (3 ounces each) strawberry
Jell-O

2 cups boiling water

1½ pounds fresh or frozen
strawberries

1. For the crust: Preheat the oven to 400°F.

2. In a large bowl, stir together the pretzels, sugar,
and cinnamon. Drizzle with the butter and toss to
coat. Press evenly into the bottom of 9 x 13-inch
baking pan. Bake until firm and lightly browned,
8 to 10 minutes. Cool to room temperature.

3. For the topping: In another large bowl, with an
electric mixer at high speed, beat the cream cheese
and sugar until smooth. Fold in the whipped
topping with a rubber spatula. Spread over the
crust.

4. Pour the Jell-O into a large bowl. Add the boiling
water and stir to dissolve. Stir in the strawberries.
Refrigerate until the mixture begins to set and
has the consistency of uncooked egg whites, about
20 minutes with fresh berries and 10 minutes for
frozen.

5. Spoon the strawberry gelatin over the whipped
topping mixture. Refrigerate until the gelatin sets,
at least 4 hours. Serve chilled.

 *A Note from Miss Kay*

*There's always room for Jell-O, as the ad used to say! This dish is as pretty as it is delicious and adds
the perfect touch of lightness to any celebration.*

Old-Fashioned Country Lemonade

■ *Makes 1½ quarts*

1 cup sugar

1 cup water

1 cup fresh lemon juice (4 to 6 lemons)

4 cups ice water

Ice

Lemon slices or wedges, for garnish

1. In a small saucepan, combine the sugar and 1 cup water and bring to a boil, stirring until the sugar dissolves. Pour into a serving pitcher. Stir in the lemon juice. Stir in the ice water.

2. Refrigerate until chilled. Serve over ice, garnished with the lemon slices.

 *A Note from Miss Kay*

Roll the lemons back and forth on the countertop while pressing them with the heel of your hand to release more juice. Of course, there are lots of lemonade mixes in the stores, but nothing beats homemade.

- 8 -

Picnics and Summer Fun

Celebrated on Any Beautiful Day

• • • • •

Kissing a man with a beard is a lot like going to a picnic.
You don't mind going through a little bush to get there!

—MINNIE PEARL

There is a time for everything,

and a season for every activity under the heavens.

—ECCLESIASTES 3:1 NIV

Recipes for Picnics and Summer Fun

Jep and his sweet family enjoy a family picnic.

Celebrating the Outdoors

I wanted to include a chapter on the outdoors because so much of our life has been dependent on it. Phil went to college and studied to be a teacher, but the outdoors kept calling him. After a few years of teaching, he told me that he was going to catch fish and hunt for a living. I seriously thought we would starve to death, but as it turns out, Phil was good at it; and we have been blessed by living "off the creation" the Almighty gave us.

You probably aren't going to fish and hunt for a living, but you can still appreciate the outdoors. We live in Louisiana, so that means there's plenty of critters, heat, and humidity. Sometimes the grandkids will want to go for a walk and I steer them toward reading a book and painting me a picture because it's just too hot to go outside. But on those good days, I love living deep on the river in northeastern Louisiana. From my doorstep, I can see the water wind around the corner of our property and hear the sounds from a motor as a fishing boat makes its way down the Ouachita River. Phil and Si remember playing on the river just like Huckleberry Finn when they were boys. And my boys loved to fish right out their back door as they were growing up.

Once we took the boys camping. We pitched our tent and built a fire; then we sat around the campfire

Jase and I enjoying an outdoor party for Sadie's sixteenth birthday.

talking for hours. Phil and I went to sleep in the tent and told the boys to come inside soon, but when we got up the next morning, we found the boys sound asleep right by the fire. They loved being outdoors so much that even the tent was too confining.

You might live in an area where you wake up to a mountain or a sandy beach, or you might live in apartment with a potted plant in your windowsill. Wherever you live, look for what God created. Seeing and appreciating God's creation teaches us to see and appreciate Him.

There's a wonderful book in the Bible called Job. It's the story of a man who was afflicted with almost every possible tragedy. When his judgmental "friends" accuse him of not understanding the ways of God, he replies with these great words in Job 12:7–11: "But ask the animals what they think—let them teach you; let the birds tell you what's going on. Put your ear to the earth—learn the basics. Listen—the fish in the ocean will tell you their stories. Isn't it clear that they all know and agree that God is sovereign, that he holds all things in his hand—every living soul, yes, every breathing creature? Isn't this all just common sense, as common as the sense of taste?" (The Message) Job knew that by observing creation, we can learn much about the Creator.

The boys get a ukulele lesson in Hawaii.

Picnics are a great way to celebrate God's beautiful creation. There's something about spreading a blanket on the ground and opening up a sack of food, even if it's just a peanut butter sandwich and a bag of chips. We can all learn a lesson from Job and let the birds teach us and the fish tell us their story, while we celebrate all of God's great outdoors!

Onion Dip

Makes about 3 cups

1 tablespoon butter
1 tablespoon extra-virgin olive oil
2 large yellow onions, diced (about 4 cups)
2 cups sour cream
1 cup mayonnaise
½ teaspoon celery seeds
½ teaspoon onion powder
½ teaspoon garlic powder
1 teaspoon kosher salt
1 teaspoon Worcestershire sauce
¼ teaspoon cayenne
¼ teaspoon ground white pepper
Potato chips, for serving

1. Heat the butter and oil in a large skillet over medium-high heat. Add the onions and stir to coat. Cover the skillet and cook until the onions wilt, about 5 minutes. Uncover and cook, stirring occasionally, until the liquid cooks away and the onions start to brown on the bottom, about 10 minutes. Continue cooking until the onions are a deep golden brown and very soft, about 20 minutes more. The onions are more likely to scorch as they get darker, so stir often during the last few minutes of cooking. Remove from the heat and let cool to room temperature.

2. In a large bowl, whisk together the sour cream, mayonnaise, celery seeds, onion powder, garlic powder, salt, Worcestershire sauce, cayenne, and white pepper. Stir in the cooled onions. Cover and refrigerate until chilled. Serve with chips.

 *A Note from Miss Kay*

This recipe may seem difficult because of the long list of ingredients, but it's not hard at all! Just mix, refrigerate, and serve!

Quick Refrigerator Pickles

■ *Makes about 4 cups*

3 cups thinly sliced pickling
    cucumbers (about 2 pounds)
1 cup thinly sliced red onion
1 cup distilled white vinegar
2 tablespoons sugar
2 teaspoons pickling spice
2 teaspoons salt

1. In a large bowl, toss together the cucumbers and onions.

2. In a small saucepan, combine the vinegar, sugar, pickling spice, and salt and bring to a simmer over medium heat, stirring until the sugar and salt dissolve. Pour the hot brine over the cucumber mixture, making sure they are submerged. Let cool to room temperature.

3. Spoon the cucumber mixture into jars. Cover and refrigerate until chilled. Store covered and refrigerated for up to 1 month.

 *A Note from Miss Kay*

If you're new to canning or pickling, this is a good place to start. After you make them, you have a whole month to eat them!

Ham Salad

■ *Makes about 4 cups*

3 cups finely chopped baked ham
    (1 pound)
¼ cup finely chopped onion
¼ cup finely chopped celery
¼ cup sweet pickle relish
1 cup mayonnaise
1 tablespoon yellow mustard
2 hard-cooked eggs, finely chopped
    (optional, see Tip on page 75)
Salt and black pepper

1. In a large bowl, stir together the ham, onion, celery, relish, mayonnaise, mustard, and eggs (if using). Season with salt and pepper to taste.

2. Cover and refrigerate until lightly chilled.

 *A Note from Miss Kay*

You can serve this on sandwiches or with crackers. If you use a food processor to chop the ham, cut the ham into 1-inch chunks before putting it in the processor. Pulse until the ham is chopped. If you turn on the machine and let it run, the ham quickly turns into mushy paste.

Cornbread Salad

Makes 12 to 16 servings

1 packet (1 ounce) ranch dressing mix

2 cups sour cream

1 cup mayonnaise

6 cups crumbled cornbread, divided

1 cup crumbled crisp-cooked bacon
(from about ½ pound raw), divided

2 cans (15 ounces each) pinto beans,
drained and rinsed, divided

2 cans (15 ounces each) whole
kernel corn, drained and rinsed,
or 3½ cups thawed frozen corn
kernels, divided

1 cup diced green bell pepper, divided

1 cup chopped green onions
(scallions), divided

3 cups seeded and diced tomatoes,
divided

2 cups (8 ounces) grated sharp
cheddar cheese, divided

1. In a small bowl, whisk together the dressing mix, sour cream, and mayonnaise.

2. In the bottom of a tall glass bowl, spread half of the cornbread. Layer in half the bacon, beans, corn, bell pepper, green onions, tomatoes, and cheese. Drizzle with half of the dressing mixture. Repeat layers.

3. Cover and refrigerate until chilled, at least 4 hours and preferably overnight.

 *A Note from Miss Kay*

Another great recipe to do ahead of time. Cornbread is a favorite in the South, and this recipe will be a crowd-pleaser for sure.

Macaroni Salad

16 ounces elbow macaroni (4 cups)

1½ cups mayonnaise

¼ cup distilled white vinegar

1 teaspoon mustard powder, such as Coleman's

1 tablespoon sugar

2 teaspoons salt, or to taste

½ teaspoon black pepper

1 medium onion, finely chopped (about 2 cups)

2 celery stalks, thinly sliced (about 1 cup)

1 green bell pepper, chopped (about 1 cup)

1 yellow, orange, or red bell pepper, chopped (about 1 cup)

1 large carrot, finely chopped or grated (about ½ cup)

1. In a large pot of boiling salted water, cook the macaroni according to package directions. Drain and pour into a large bowl.

2. In a small bowl, stir together the mayonnaise, vinegar, mustard powder, sugar, salt, and pepper. Pour over the warm macaroni and stir to coat. Cool to room temperature, stirring occasionally.

3. Stir in the onion, celery, green bell pepper, yellow bell pepper, and carrot. Cover and refrigerate until chilled, at least 4 hours and preferably overnight. Just before serving, stir well and check the seasoning.

 *A Note from Miss Kay*

This is the perfect dish for a picnic or family reunion. It can be done ahead of time, giving you plenty of time to do other things before the celebration.

Cold Oven-Fried Chicken Drumsticks

■ *Makes 6 servings*

3 tablespoons butter, melted
½ cup baking mix, such as Bisquick
1 teaspoon poultry seasoning
½ teaspoon paprika
2 teaspoons salt
½ teaspoon black pepper
12 chicken drumsticks, skin removed

1. Preheat the oven to 450°F. Pour the melted butter evenly over the bottom of 9 x13-inch baking dish.

2. In a shallow dish, whisk together the baking mix, poultry seasoning, paprika, salt, and pepper. Lightly and evenly coat the drumsticks. Arrange the drumsticks in single layer in the baking dish.

3. Bake for 40 minutes, rotating the drumsticks a quarter-turn every 10 minutes with tongs so that they brown evenly on all sides. Let cool to room temperature and then refrigerate until chilled— although these are also great served warm.

 *A Note from Miss Kay*

Calling all new cooks! This one is too easy to not *do. Everyone will love these tasty drumsticks!*

Mamaw Kay's Cookie Bars

■ *Makes 24 servings*

1 stick (¼ pound) butter

1½ cups graham cracker crumbs

1 cup semisweet chocolate chips

1 cup butterscotch chips

1 cup chopped pecans

1 can (14 ounces) sweetened condensed milk, such as Eagle Brand

1⅓ cups sweetened flaked coconut

1. Preheat the oven to 350°F.

2. Put the butter in a 9 x 13-inch baking pan and place in the oven until melted. Swirl to coat bottom and sides of pan.

3. Sprinkle the crumbs over the melted butter and pat evenly. Sprinkle the chocolate chips over the crumbs, then the butterscotch chips, and then the pecans. Drizzle the condensed milk over the top. Sprinkle with the coconut.

4. Bake until golden brown, about 25 minutes. Cool to room temperature on a wire cooling rack before cutting.

 *A Note from Miss Kay*

This is a great cookie. It has several wonderful cookie ingredients all together. A favorite of everyone!

Cream Cheese Brownies

Makes 8 to 10 servings

1 box brownie mix (I use Ghirardelli
  Double Chocolate)

Ingredients listed on brownie mix
  package for preparing batter

8 ounces cream cheese, at room
  temperature

⅓ cup sugar

½ teaspoon vanilla extract

1 large egg yolk

1. Preheat the oven and prepare the brownie batter according to the package directions. Scrape the batter into a 9-inch square baking pan.

2. In a large bowl, with an electric mixer on medium speed (or by hand with a wooden spoon), combine the cream cheese, sugar, vanilla, and egg yolk until smooth. Spoon big dollops over the brownie batter and use a chopstick or butter knife to pull swirls through the batter.

3. Bake according to package directions. Let cool for at least 15 minutes before serving warm or at room temperature. The cooler they are, the easier they are to cut and remove from the pan.

Willie and Martin get in the water for some redneck fun.

A Note from Miss Kay

This is a delicious twist to the traditional brownie mix. Everyone will love it.

Watermelonade

1½ pounds watermelon, seeded and coarsely chopped (about 4 cups)

2 tablespoons chopped fresh mint

4 tablespoons sugar, or to taste

Juice of 1 lime

Thin lime wedges, fresh mint sprigs, or small slices of watermelon, for garnish

1. Puree the watermelon, mint, sugar, and lime juice in a blender until the mint is very finely chopped, about 1 minute.

2. Refrigerate until chilled. Before serving, garnish with lime and mint or watermelon slices.

A Note from Miss Kay

Watermelon is a must for a picnic and this watermelon drink is too! Your whole family will love this summertime treat!

- *9* -

Grandparents' Day

Celebrated on the First Sunday after Labor Day

· · · ·

If you're lucky enough to still have grandparents,

visit them, cherish them and celebrate them while you can.

—REGINA BRETT

That precious memory triggers another:

your honest faith—and what a rich faith it is,

handed down from your grandmother Lois

to your mother Eunice, and now to you!

—2 TIMOTHY 1:5 THE MESSAGE

Recipes for Loving on the Grandparents in Your Life

Sadie and her Papaw Phil share a special moment out on the water.

Celebrating Grandparents

There's an old joke that says if I knew grandchildren would be so much fun, I would have had them first! I have to agree; I love my grandchildren. And having grandchildren made me appreciate my grandparents and Phil's grandparents even more. I've mentioned before that I spent most days with my grandparents while my parents managed the local grocery store. My grandfather died when I was twelve. Looking back, I'm sure I was good company for my grandmother after her husband was gone, but I really didn't think about that as a kid. Of course, now, I wish I had celebrated them more or at least had written down their wise sayings and good advice. But I remember enough of those days to pass on what I learned to my grandkids.

One of the things I remember most about my "nannie" was her love for cooking. I realize now that while Nannie was teaching me to cook, she was really teaching me to use my cooking to show love to others. Nannie was the first in our community to show up with food for any occasion, and watching her take care of others taught me that people are important and that people in crisis need help. From my grandpa, I learned to work hard at anything I do. I used to ride on the pony as he plowed the ground for the garden. My grandfather was dedicated to his family and had a job to do, so every day was "take your kid to work day" for me!

Grandparents are the glue that holds generations together. Since I didn't have my mother when my babies were born, Phil's grandmother came to help me. It was so comforting to have someone older and wiser help me take care of my new baby. I couldn't begin to count the many meals both of our grandmothers cooked for us. Now that Phil and I are grandparents to fourteen and great-grandparents to four, I see our roles as matriarch and patriarch of the family as important ones. This is biblical. Most of us skip over the long genealogy chapters in the Bible, but I believe they're listed so we can understand the importance of heritage. I want my children and grandchildren to be able to depend on me for a meal if they need it, and also for good advice and a strong example. Phil and I want to continue to lead our family, but not in a smothering way. We know that all of our sons are raising their own families, and our job is to support them in any way we can but never to take over their jobs.

Some people think that Grandparents' Day was created by card and florist companies as another way to make money; but the truth is that President Jimmy Carter signed it in as a national holiday in 1978. I have to admit, as much as our family celebrates *everything*, we still don't always remember this one. So I'm here to change that! We need to honor the more than 70 million grandparents in America today. It's always the Sunday following Labor Day, so it's not too hard to remember. Did you know that Grandparents' Day even has an official song and flower? Seriously, you might want to look it up just before you order the cake, buy the flowers, pick out a card, cook a fabulous meal, and celebrate those amazing older folks who are a vital part of our families, our churches, and our communities. Enjoy!

Missy directs Grandparents' Day at school. Here she is with Mia.

Confetti Corn

■ *Makes 6 to 8 servings*

3 tablespoons bacon drippings or butter

1 small red onion, diced

1 red bell pepper, diced

1 orange bell pepper, diced

4 cups fresh or thawed frozen corn kernels

2 garlic cloves, finely chopped

2 teaspoons fresh thyme leaves

2 teaspoons fresh marjoram or oregano leaves

2 teaspoons salt, or to taste

Black pepper

1. In a large skillet, melt the drippings over medium-high heat. Stir in the onion and bell pepper and cook, stirring occasionally, until tender, about 5 minutes.

2. Stir in the corn, garlic, thyme, marjoram, salt, and pepper to taste. Cook, stirring occasionally, until the corn is just done, about 5 minutes. Check the seasoning and serve hot.

I love my little grand-girls!

A Note from Miss Kay

You can't beat fresh corn in the summer, but this dish is also perfect for fall. It's colorful and delicious!

Cheesy Jalapeño Cornbread Muffins

■ *Makes 12 muffins*

Cooking spray
1½ cups cornmeal
1½ cups all-purpose flour
2 tablespoons sugar
1½ teaspoons baking powder
½ teaspoon baking soda
2 cups buttermilk
2 large eggs
1 stick (¼ pound) butter, melted
1 cup grated sharp cheddar or
　　Monterey jack cheese, divided
2 large jalapeño peppers, 1 finely
　　chopped and 1 cut crosswise into
　　12 rounds

1. Preheat the oven to 375°F. Mist a standard 12-cup muffin tin with cooking spray or line with paper liners.

2. In a large bowl, whisk together the cornmeal, flour, sugar, baking powder, and baking soda.

3. In a medium bowl, whisk together the buttermilk, eggs, and melted butter. Pour the buttermilk mixture into the cornmeal mixture and stir only until blended.

4. Stir in ⅔ cup of the cheese and the chopped jalapeño. Spoon the batter into the muffin cups. Sprinkle the remaining ⅓ cup cheese over the muffins. Place 1 jalapeño slice on top of each muffin.

5. Bake until golden brown on top and a wooden pick inserted into the centers comes out clean, about 25 minutes. Remove the muffins from the tin to cool for 5 minutes before serving.

 *A Note from Miss Kay*

If you don't have fresh jalapeños, pickled jalapeño slices from a jar work fine. I use Aunt Jemima cornmeal, but any will do.

Meaty Chili

Makes 8 servings

2 tablespoons vegetable oil

12 ounces ground beef

12 ounces ground pork

2 pounds trimmed chuck roast, cut into 1-inch cubes

2 large onions, chopped (about 6 cups)

3 garlic cloves, chopped

6 tablespoons chili powder

1 tablespoon ground cumin

1 tablespoon dried oregano

2 teaspoons salt, or to taste

3 cups beef broth

1 can (28 ounces) fire-roasted diced tomatoes

2 cans (15 ounces each) pinto beans, drained and rinsed

2 tablespoons cornmeal, masa harina, or corn flour

¼ cup water

Grated cheese, such as cheddar or Monterey Jack, and sour cream, for serving

1. In a Dutch oven, heat the oil over medium-high heat. Add the ground beef and pork and cook, stirring often, until the meat is browned with no traces of pink, about 10 minutes. Scrape into a large bowl.

2. Working in batches, add the chuck roast to the pot and cook, turning as needed, until the pieces are seared and browned on all sides. Add to the bowl with the ground meats.

3. Add the onion to the Dutch oven and cook, stirring often, until tender, about 5 minutes.

4. Add the garlic, chili powder, cumin, oregano, and salt and cook, stirring constantly, for 2 minutes. Reduce the heat if the spices begin to scorch.

5. Stir in the broth and tomatoes. Return the browned meats to the pot. Cover and simmer, stirring occasionally, until the cubes of chuck are very tender, about 1 hour.

6. Stir in the beans. Return to a simmer. In a small bowl, whisk together the cornmeal and water. Add the cornmeal mixture to the pot, stir well, and simmer until the chili thickens slightly, about 30 minutes. Check the seasoning.

7. Serve hot, topped with the cheese and sour cream.

 *A Note from Miss Kay*

Chili always tastes best when made a day ahead, refrigerated overnight, and reheated the next day.

Slow-Cooker Hot Spiced Apple Cider

Makes 2 quarts

2 quarts unfiltered apple cider

5 whole allspice berries

5 whole cloves

Two 3-inch cinnamon sticks

Juice of 1 orange

Juice of 1 lemon

1 orange studded with 2 tablespoons
   whole cloves, for garnish, optional

1. Pour the cider into a 4-quart slow cooker. Add the allspice berries, cloves, and cinnamon sticks. Cover and cook on the low setting for 3 hours.

2. Just before serving, discard the spices. Stir in the orange juice and lemon juice. Float the clove-studded orange in the cider for garnish, if you like.

Papaw Phil surrounded by the grandkids.

 *A Note from Miss Kay*

If you don't have a slow cooker, you can keep this warm over low heat in a large pot on the stove. Either way, your kitchen will smell wonderful.

Broccoli Salad

Makes 8 servings

10 ounces fresh broccoli crowns, broken into bite-size florets (about 6 cups)

½ cup finely diced red onion

½ cup sunflower or pumpkin seeds

½ cup dried cranberries

½ cup crumbled crisp-cooked bacon (from about ¼ pound raw)

¾ cup mayonnaise

2 tablespoons apple cider vinegar

½ teaspoon mustard powder, such as Coleman's

½ teaspoon lemon pepper

1 teaspoon salt

¼ cup sugar

1. In a large serving bowl, toss together the broccoli, onion, sunflower seeds, cranberries, and bacon.

2. In a small bowl, whisk together the mayonnaise, vinegar, mustard powder, lemon pepper, salt, and sugar. Let stand 5 minutes to allow the sugar to dissolve, then whisk again. Pour over the broccoli mixture and toss to coat.

3. Cover and refrigerate until chilled before serving, at least 2 hours and up to overnight. Stir well just before serving.

 *A Note from Miss Kay*

This salad is the best light touch with chili (see page 168) or stew. A great way to get those veggies in!

Venison Stew

■ *Makes 8 to 10 servings*

2 pounds venison roast, cut into
   2-inch chunks

2 teaspoons salt, plus more to taste

1 teaspoon black pepper, plus more
   to taste

3 tablespoons bacon grease or
   vegetable oil, divided

1 large onion, finely chopped (about
   3 cups)

2 celery stalks, finely chopped (about
   1 cup)

¼ cup ketchup

1 tablespoon Worcestershire sauce

1 teaspoon hot sauce

1½ to 2 cups beef broth

1 pound small white potatoes, halved
   (or quartered if larger than a golf
   ball)

1 pound large carrots, cut into 3-inch
   lengths

¼ cup cornstarch dissolved in ¼ cup
   cold water (optional)

Sprigs of rosemary, for garnish
   (optional)

1. Season the venison chunks with the salt and pepper to taste. In a Dutch oven or large pot, heat the bacon grease over medium-high heat. Working in batches, add the meat to the pot and cook undisturbed until the bottoms are seared and deeply browned. Turn the meat with tongs to sear all sides, 2 to 3 minutes per side. Move the browned meat to a large bowl.

2. Add the onion and celery to the pot. Stir to scrape up the browned bits from the bottom of the pan. If the mixture begins to stick or scorch, add ¼ cup water and stir well. Cook, stirring often, until tender, about 5 minutes.

3. Stir in the ketchup, Worcestershire sauce, hot sauce, and 1½ cups broth. Return the meat and any accumulated juices to the pot. The cooking liquid should barely cover the venison, so add more broth if needed. Bring to a boil, reduce the heat, cover tightly, and cook at a bare simmer until the meat is so tender that you can easily pull off a piece with tongs or a spoon, about 2 hours. Don't let the liquid boil.

5. Stir in the potatoes and carrots. Simmer until tender, about 30 minutes. The cooking liquid will be thin, but flavorful. If you prefer gravy-style liquid, stir in the cornstarch and water mixture and cook, stirring constantly, until bubbling and slightly thickened.

6. Check the seasoning and serve hot. Garnish with a few sprigs of rosemary.

 *A Note from Miss Kay*

For the best flavor, cool the stew, cover, and refrigerate overnight. Discard any fat that solidifies on top. Reheat gently before serving. We always have plenty of venison, but if you can't get it, beef chuck roast makes a great substitute.

Apple Crisp

Makes 10 to 12 servings

Filling

3 pounds baking apples, peeled, cored, and cut into 1-inch-thick wedges

Juice and finely grated zest of 1 large lemon

½ cup packed light brown sugar

½ teaspoon ground cinnamon

Topping

1 cup all-purpose flour

1 teaspoon baking powder

1 cup packed light brown sugar

½ cup rolled oats

½ teaspoon ground cinnamon

½ teaspoon ground nutmeg

1 stick (¼ pound) butter, cut into small cubes and chilled

1. For the filling: Preheat the oven to 350°F. Butter a 9 x 13-inch baking dish.

2. Place the apple wedges in a large bowl. Sprinkle with the lemon juice and toss. In a small bowl, stir together the lemon zest, brown sugar, and cinnamon. Sprinkle over the apples and toss to coat. Pour into the baking dish.

3. For the topping: In another large bowl, whisk together the flour, baking powder, brown sugar, oats, cinnamon, and nutmeg. Work in the butter with a pastry blender or your fingertips until the mixture is crumbly with a few pieces of the butter the size of green peas. Place in the freezer until the butter is firm, about 10 minutes. Sprinkle evenly over the apple mixture.

4. Bake until the topping is browned and the filling is bubbling, 50 to 60 minutes. Let cool for 30 minutes before serving.

 *A Note from Miss Kay*

Another great fall recipe! Nothing beats the smell of cinnamon coming from the kitchen on a crisp fall day.

Pumpkin Pie Dip

Makes about 4 cups

8 ounces cream cheese, at room temperature

1 can (15 ounces) pumpkin pie filling

1 teaspoon pumpkin pie spice, plus more for sprinkling

2 to 3 cups powdered sugar, sifted

Gingersnap cookies and fresh apple or pear slices, for serving

1. In a large bowl, with an electric mixer at medium speed, beat the cream cheese, pie filling, and pumpkin pie spice until smooth.

2. With the mixer at low speed, add enough powdered sugar to give the mixture the consistency of a soft dip.

3. Cover and refrigerate until chilled, at least 4 hours. Serve with the cookies and fruit.

 *A Note from Miss Kay*

This can be served as an appetizer, snack, or light dessert. It's also great for a fall wedding or baby shower.

Haystack Cookies

Makes 16 to 20

6 ounces butterscotch chips

6 ounces peanut butter chips

3 tablespoons peanut butter (regular, not all-natural)

1 can (5 ounces) chow mein noodles

1. Line a baking sheet with parchment paper.

2. In a large glass bowl, combine the butterscotch chips, peanut butter chips, and peanut butter. Microwave on 50% power in 30-second intervals until the chips begin to lose their shape. Stir until melted and smooth. Quickly fold in the chow mein noodles with a large rubber spatula.

3. While the mixture is still warm, form into small mounds (about 2 inches wide and 2 inches tall) on the lined baking sheet. Let sit at room temperature until firm. Store in an airtight container at room temperature.

 *A Note from Miss Kay*

This quick recipe has been around for a while, but it's great for fall. The colors are perfect, and the taste is rich and creamy. It's also easy to do with the grandkids.

- 10 -

Family Reunions and Potluck Meals

Celebrated Whenever Family and Friends Are Gathered Together

· · · · ·

You can achieve all the things you want to do,

but it's much better to do it with loved ones around you;

family and friends, people that you care about that can help you

on the way and can celebrate you,

and you can enjoy the journey.

—JOHN LASSETER

Celebrate everything that you and your families

have accomplished under the blessings of God, your God.

—DEUTERONOMY 12:7 THE MESSAGE

Recipes for Get-Togethers with Family and Friends

Uncle Si and his tea, enjoying a family gathering.

Celebrating Family and Friendships

One great thing about getting older is the abundance of friends you accumulate. I look back at our life and see the many people who have lived life with me and I am overwhelmed with love for them. Our first friends were naturally family. Because Phil has so many siblings, it was easy to find someone to do things with in our early years. In fact, it's well known that Uncle Si went with us everywhere! But his other siblings and their spouses were there with us, too, and we still count them as our closest friends. I have one sister (she's known as Aunt Ann), but she's several years older than I am, so our friendship didn't really develop until we were older. Now, she travels with me any chance she can and always goes with us on our beach trip. As the kids say, she's my BFF.

Bella helps me cut out duck cookies for a family picnic.

This past year we had a family reunion. We had never had a reunion on the Robertson side of the family, but the good news is we never really needed one because we all lived in the same area and saw one another often. But now that the kids and grandkids are drifting away, we realized it was time for a family reunion. Everyone came to our house, and we had a big meal together and then talked and

My sister, Ann, and me at the annual family getaway.

laughed and told stories for hours. It was everything a family reunion should be.

Beyond family, we have amazing friends from all walks of life, but mostly from our church family. These are the people who have laughed with us, cried with us, supported us, encouraged us, and stood by us through every stage of our life. A TV show and more money can bring about many changes in a person's life, but it can't bring you true friends. True friends are the ones who are with you when you don't have anything. Then when you get something, they are just happy for you, not wanting something from you.

And, yes, friendship in the South almost always starts with food. From our earliest years with our church family, we have invited people over for fish fries and shrimp boils. Many times, Phil and I will do all the cooking, but other times, everyone brings a dish or two to complete the meal. Talking over a good meal is the best way to develop a friendship. Even cleaning up after a meal adds to the friendship. Our kitchen is small, so working together takes on a new meaning. I often have a group of ladies crowded in trying to stir gravy, butter rolls, slice meat, cut up dessert, make tea, and put the ice in glasses while kids are running through the kitchen. (Did I mention the house is small?) But being together is what celebrating family and friendships is all about.

If you haven't had a chance to share a meal with those you love, today's a good day to start planning a get-together. Keep it simple, realizing it's not about the food you serve or the size of the place you gather in; it's about telling others they matter to you. Life is short. Let your friends and family know you love them by celebrating them.

Crawfish (or Shrimp) Boil

Makes 12 servings

Note: A crawfish or shrimp boil is a fun event, but it calls for some special equipment. Prepare before you start, and you'll have a great time!

1 bottle (12 ounces) hot sauce (I use Crystal)

1 pound salt

1 bottle (4 ounces) Zatarain's Concentrated Crawfish, Shrimp & Crab Boil

2 sticks (½ pound) butter

1 cup lemon juice

8 pounds fresh, live crawfish or 12 pounds large shell-on fresh shrimp

3 pounds new red potatoes, each about the size of a golf ball, scrubbed

2 pounds small onions, peeled and halved

12 ears fresh corn, halved crosswise

1. Place a 40-gallon stockpot with its insert on an outdoor gas burner. Fill the pot half full of water. Add the hot sauce, salt, concentrated boil seasoning (see Tip), butter, and lemon juice. Bring to a simmer and cook for 15 minutes.

2. Meanwhile, clean the crawfish; the shrimp come already clean (do not peel the shrimp). To clean the crawfish, hose them down while still in the mesh bag they came in until the water runs clear, about 5 minutes. Dump the crawfish or shrimp into 1 or 2 ice chests or 1 very large cooler. Fill with water and stir gently to loosen any remaining dirt. Discard any debris, dead crawfish, or crawfish with a straight tail. Let sit 5 minutes. Open the drain and let the water run out. Repeat until the water runs clear.

3. Add the potatoes and onions to the stockpot, bring to a boil, cover, and cook 10 minutes.

4. Add the corn to the pot, cover, and cook until the potatoes are tender, 10 to 15 minutes more.

5. Add the crawfish (or shrimp) to the pot, cover, and cook about 3 minutes. Turn off the heat and let sit for at least 10 minutes and up to 20 minutes. The longer the crawfish (or shrimp) soak in the cooking liquid, the spicier they'll be. (But you may want to serve immediately, and that works well too.)

6. Slowly lift the insert out of the pot and drain well. Pour the shellfish onto the table covered with newspaper. Dig in immediately.

continued on page 185

Tip: Read the back of the bottle of Zatarain's to make sure you're using the correct amount for the weight of crawfish you're going to cook. If you can't find the liquid concentrate, use Zatarain's Crawfish, Crab & Shrimp Boil in bags. There are extra-hot versions of both products.

A Note from Miss Kay

Live fresh crawfish are not available year round, and they might be hard to find outside of Louisiana—although there are companies that will ship them to you on ice. Fresh shrimp in their shells are a great substitute, and they don't require as much cleaning. Having a crawfish or shrimp boil is a big event and takes some work. It's best to eat it outdoors, but either way, cover the table with newspaper or a plastic tablecloth, then pour the crawfish or shrimp right onto the table. Be sure to have several rolls of paper towels handy and let people have at it. If you use shrimp, they can be cooked in the kitchen, but beware, the smell might linger.

Chicken Enchiladas

■ *Makes 4 to 6 servings*

Cooking spray

2 cups chopped cooked chicken

4 cups (16 ounces) grated Mexican blend cheese, divided

2 cups sour cream

1 can (4 ounces) chopped green chiles

½ cup very finely chopped onion

2 cups green chile enchilada sauce, divided

Eight 8-inch flour tortillas

1. Preheat the oven to 350°F. Mist a 9 x 13-inch baking dish with cooking spray.

2. In a large bowl, stir together the chicken, 2 cups of the cheese, the sour cream, green chiles, onion, and 1 cup of the enchilada sauce.

3. Fill each tortilla with about ½ cup of the chicken mixture. Roll up and place seam-side down in the baking dish. Pour the remaining 1 cup enchilada sauce over the top. Sprinkle with the remaining 2 cups cheese.

4. Cover with foil and bake for 20 minutes. Uncover and continue baking until the cheese is bubbling and browned in spots, about 10 minutes more. Serve hot.

A Note from Miss Kay

Everyone needs a good enchilada recipe. Our family loves this one. This recipe is easy to make, and you can use that tasty, store-bought rotisserie chicken to save time.

Fried Catfish

Makes 8 servings

1½ cups corn flour or cornmeal

1½ cups all-purpose flour

2 teaspoons Old Bay seasoning

4 teaspoons kosher salt, plus more
   for sprinkling

½ teaspoon black pepper

½ teaspoon paprika

¼ teaspoon cayenne

1 cup buttermilk

1 quart peanut oil, for deep-frying

8 large catfish fillets

1. In a shallow bowl, whisk together the corn flour, flour, Old Bay, salt, pepper, paprika, and cayenne. Pour the buttermilk into a second shallow bowl.

3. Pour the oil to a depth of 4 inches in a deep-fryer or Dutch oven. Heat to 375°F on a deep-fry thermometer over medium-high heat. Adjust the heat as needed to maintain 375°F throughout the cooking process. Line a wire cooling rack with paper towels.

4. Dip the fillets into the buttermilk, letting the excess drip back into the bowl. Coat the fillets lightly and evenly in the corn flour mixture. Set aside in a single layer while the oil heats.

5. Slip the coated fillets into the hot oil. Do not add more fillets at once than can float freely. Fry until the coating is a deep golden brown and the fillets float, about 4 minutes. Transfer the cooked fillets to the lined cooling rack to drain. Sprinkle the hot fillets immediately with a little more salt.

 *A Note from Miss Kay*

Corn flour is very finely ground cornmeal. You can sometimes find it labeled as seasoned fish fry, such as Zatarain's. If you use "seasoned fish fry," omit the Old Bay, salt, paprika, and cayenne from this recipe as it already has those seasonings in there. You shouldn't have any trouble finding these ingredients.

Spinach Madeleine

Makes 6 servings

2 packages (10 ounces each) frozen chopped spinach, thawed

5 tablespoons butter, divided

2 tablespoons all-purpose flour

2 tablespoons very finely chopped onion

2 tablespoons very finely chopped jalapeño pepper

½ cup evaporated milk

1 teaspoon Worcestershire sauce

½ teaspoon salt

½ teaspoon black pepper

1 teaspoon garlic powder

6 ounces original or Mexican Velveeta, cut into small cubes

¼ cup fine dried bread crumbs

1. Cook the spinach according to package directions. Drain well in a fine-mesh sieve set over a bowl, pressing firmly with a spoon to remove as much liquid as possible. Set aside ¼ cup liquid and discard the rest.

2. In a medium saucepan, melt 4 tablespoons of the butter over medium-low heat. Add the flour and whisk until smooth. Whisk in the onion and jalapeño and cook, whisking constantly, for 2 minutes. Do not let the flour brown at all.

3. Whisk in the reserved spinach liquid, evaporated milk, and Worcestershire sauce. Cook, whisking slowly, until the mixture thickens and comes just to a boil, about 3 minutes. Remove from the heat and stir in the salt, pepper, and garlic powder. Add the Velveeta and stir until melted and smooth. Stir in the spinach. Pour into a serving dish.

4. This can be served now, but for best flavor, cool, cover, and refrigerate overnight. Reheat gently over low heat. Just before serving, melt the remaining 1 tablespoon butter and toss with the bread crumbs. Sprinkle the bread crumb mixture over the top and serve warm.

 *A Note from Miss Kay*

This recipe was made famous by the equally famous River Road Recipes, *a cookbook from the Junior League of Baton Rouge. Some of the ingredients listed in the original version of the recipe are no longer available, but the recipe is too good to let go, so home cooks have adapted the recipe over the years.*

Tater Tot Casserole

■ *Makes 8 servings*

Cooking spray

2 pounds lean ground beef

2 cups frozen mixed vegetables, thawed

1 teaspoon salt

¼ teaspoon black pepper

2 teaspoons Italian seasoning

1 can (10.75 ounces) condensed cream of mushroom soup

½ cup sour cream

2 cups (8 ounces) shredded cheddar cheese, divided

1 bag (32 ounces) tater tots

1. Preheat the oven to 350°F. Mist a 2½-quart baking dish with cooking spray.

2. In a large skillet, cook the ground beef over medium-high heat until browned with no traces of pink, about 10 minutes. Stir in the mixed vegetables, salt, pepper, and Italian seasoning. Cook for 5 minutes, stirring often. Transfer to the baking dish.

3. In a medium bowl, whisk together the soup and sour cream. Spread over the beef mixture. Sprinkle with 1 cup of the cheese. Spread the tater tots over the cheese.

4. Bake for 40 minutes. Sprinkle the remaining 1 cup cheese over the top and continue baking until the cheese is bubbling and browned in spots, about 10 minutes more. Serve hot.

October is all about dressing up!

 *A Note from Miss Kay*

This all-in-one meal is packed with flavor and is an easy way to feed a family or group of friends on a busy night. Our grandkids love this dish, so you might even sneak a vegetable in them.

Shrimp Creole

Makes 8 servings

1 stick (¼ pound) butter

1 medium onion, chopped (about 2 cups)

2 celery stalks, chopped (about 1 cup)

1 green bell pepper, chopped (about 1 cup)

1 tablespoon tomato paste

4 large garlic cloves, chopped (about 1 tablespoon)

1 tablespoon Creole seasoning blend, such as Tony Chachere's

1 teaspoon salt, or to taste

¼ teaspoon cayenne, or to taste

2 cups seafood stock or chicken broth

1 can (28 ounces) whole tomatoes in thick puree, chopped with their juices

1 tablespoon Worcestershire sauce

2 bay leaves

1 tablespoon fresh thyme leaves

1 teaspoon hot sauce, or to taste

2½ pounds large (16/20 count) fresh shrimp, peeled and deveined

4 to 6 cups hot, freshly cooked long-grain white rice

¼ cup thinly sliced green onions (scallions)

¼ cup finely chopped flat-leaf parsley

Hot sauce, for serving

1. In a large pot, melt the butter over medium-high heat. Add the onion, celery, and bell pepper and cook, stirring often, until tender, about 5 minutes.

2. Stir in the tomato paste, garlic, Creole seasoning, salt, and cayenne. Cook, stirring, for 2 minutes.

3. Add the stock, tomatoes, Worcestershire sauce, bay leaves, thyme, and hot sauce. Bring to a boil, reduce the heat, and simmer for 30 minutes, stirring occasionally.

4. Stir in the shrimp and simmer only until opaque, about 4 minutes. Discard the bay leaves, and check the seasoning.

5. Serve hot over rice, sprinkled with the green onions and parsley. Pass a bottle of hot sauce at the table.

 *A Note from Miss Kay*

There are as many Shrimp Creole recipes in Louisiana as there are parishes. This is just one of them, but it's one our family likes. Enjoy!

Frosted Butter Cookies

■ *Makes about 4 dozen cookies, depending on size and shape*

Cookies

1¼ cups powdered sugar, sifted
2¼ sticks (½ pound plus
   2 tablespoons) unsalted butter,
   at room temperature
2 large egg yolks
1 teaspoon salt
½ teaspoon almond extract
½ teaspoon vanilla extract
2¾ cups all-purpose flour

Frosting

4 large pasteurized egg whites
½ teaspoon vanilla extract
½ teaspoon almond extract
4 cups powdered sugar, sifted
1 to 6 teaspoons milk, if needed
Food coloring gel (optional)
Sprinkles, jimmies, sanding sugar
   (optional)

1. For the cookies: In a large bowl, with an electric mixer at high speed, beat the powdered sugar, butter, egg yolks, salt, almond extract, and vanilla extract until smooth.

2. Add the flour and beat on low speed until large clumps of dough form. The dough will look too dry at first, so be patient.

3. Pour the dough clumps onto a large sheet of plastic wrap. Gather into a ball and flatten into a disk. Cover with a second sheet of plastic wrap and roll to ⅛-inch thickness. It will be a very large piece of dough. Slide onto a rimmed baking sheet to keep the dough flat and refrigerate until firm, at least 2 hours and up to overnight.

4. Preheat the oven to 350°F. Line a baking sheet with parchment paper.

5. Discard the plastic wrap. Place the dough on a lightly floured surface. Stamp out cookies with cutters of your choice. Simple shapes with clean edges work best. Arrange the cookies on the lined baking sheet, spacing them about 1 inch apart. Bake until golden brown on the edges, 12 to 15 minutes, depending on size. Cool the cookies on the baking sheet.

6. For the frosting: In a large glass or metal bowl, with an electric mixer at low speed, beat the egg whites until frothy. Beat in the vanilla and almond extract. With the mixer running, add the powdered sugar 1 cup at a time. Beat on low speed until smooth. Increase the speed to high and beat until stiff, shiny peaks form, 5 to 7 minutes. The

recipe continued on next page

A Note from Miss Kay

This is a great recipe for any occasion. You might want to look for pasteurized eggs at the grocery store. Pasteurization makes the uncooked egg white safe to eat. Use them as you would regular eggs. If you don't own a pastry bag, use a plastic freezer bag. Work the icing to the corner, clip off a tiny corner, and slide a decorator tip into place. If you don't have a decorator tip, you can squeeze simple lines of frosting directly from the freezer bag.

frosting should be fairly thick, but spreadable, so add a little milk to thin it if necessary. If you plan to pipe the frosting onto the cookies with a pastry bag fitted with a decorator tip, thin with enough milk to make it flow through the tip when the bag is squeezed.

7. Tint the frosting with food coloring, if desired. The gel is very concentrated, so add a tiny bit at a time and mix it in well before adding more.

8. Quickly frost the cooled cookies. If using, add sprinkles or other decorations while the frosting is moist. Let sit until the frosting hardens before storing the cookies in an airtight container at room temperature.

Peach Nehi Ice Cream

▪ *Makes 1 quart*

1 can (14 ounces) sweetened condensed milk, such as Eagle Brand
3 cups finely chopped fresh peeled peaches (or use thawed frozen peaches or drained canned peaches)
4 cups peach-flavored soft drink, such as Nehi

1. In a large bowl, whisk together the condensed milk and peaches. Slowly stir in the soft drink. Cover and refrigerate until very cold, at least 4 hours.

2. Pour the mixture into a 1½-quart ice cream freezer and process according to the manufacturer's instructions. The mixture will have the consistency of a thick milkshake. For ice cream firm enough to scoop, spoon into a very clean airtight container and freeze until firm.

A Note from Miss Kay

This recipe is proportioned for a 1½-quart countertop electric ice cream freezer. If you are using a larger, crank-style freezer, increase the recipe to fill it properly according to the manufacturer's directions.

A table full of food says it all— celebrate with family and friends!

A smiling grandmother— with my older grandkids.

Punch Bowl Cake

■ *Makes 16 to 20 servings*

2 boxes (5.1 ounces each) instant vanilla pudding mix

5 cups whole milk

8 cups plain pound cake cut into 1-inch cubes (from about two 8 x 4-inch loaves)

2 cans (21 ounces each) cherry pie filling (I use Lucky Leaf)

2 cans (20 ounces each) crushed pineapple, drained

8 ounces sweetened flaked coconut

1 container (16 ounces) frozen whipped topping, such as Cool Whip, thawed

¼ cup chopped pecans

1. In a large bowl, whisk together the pudding mixes and milk. Refrigerate until partially set, about 5 minutes.

2. Spread half of the cake cubes in the bottom of a large glass bowl. Spoon half of the pudding over the cake. Layer in 1 can of pie filling, 1 can of pineapple, then half of the coconut. Repeat the layers.

3. Top with the whipped topping and sprinkle with the pecans.

4. Cover and refrigerate overnight. Serve chilled.

Lily, Aslyn (a cousin on Korie's side), and Bella perform on Grandparents' Day.

🦆 *A Note from Miss Kay*

You don't have to use a real punch bowl to make this cake, but be sure to use a large glass serving bowl, such as a trifle bowl, so all those tempting layers show.

- *11* -

Thanksgiving

Celebrated on the Final Thursday in November

■ ■ ■ ■ ■

There is one day that is ours.

Thanksgiving Day is the one day that is purely American.

—O. HENRY

Hallelujah! I give thanks to God

with everything I've got—

Whenever good people gather, and in the congregation.

—PSALMS 111:1 THE MESSAGE

Recipes for a
Special Day of Thanks

Thanksgiving is a wonderful time to be with family. Here, Missy helps prepare a salad.

Celebrating and Being Thankful

By now you've figured out that I love every holiday. I guess you could say I never met a holiday I didn't like. I'm a people person, and holidays give people a reason to gather up. And I love to gather up!

One of the reasons I love Thanksgiving is that it doesn't involve anything much except eating and being together. Just good food, a TV for sports lovers, and an afternoon nap. Love it! But there is one Thanksgiving that has special meaning to me, and that's the one after Phil turned his life around and came back to our family. It was the first holiday after he returned, and I remember how thankful I was that our family was back together.

But sometimes, joyful occasions can be sad—like after the death of a loved one. The holidays can remind us that our loved one is missing. But even after loss, there are reasons to celebrate, and that's what Thanksgiving is all about. One year, someone in Korie's family made a big turkey out of poster paper, then cut feathers out of different colors of construction paper. Each person attending the Thanksgiving lunch wrote what they were thankful for on a construction paper feather and taped the feather to the turkey. It was a beautiful way to see everyone's blessings.

There's evidence of a Thanksgiving celebration dating back to the pilgrims in 1621; but on October 3, 1789, President George Washington proclaimed that the people of the United States would observe "a day of public thanksgiving and prayer" on Thursday, November 26 of that year. It was still many years, like one hundred, before the holiday was well established. And credit for that goes to Sarah Josepha

Hale. She was the editor of a women's magazine. She started printing stories and recipes and writing influential people like governors and senators to get the holiday more attention. Her hard work paid off, and after thirty-six years of petitioning, on October 3, 1863, President Abraham Lincoln proclaimed that Thanksgiving would be a national holiday to be observed on the final Thursday of November. I'm thankful for Sarah's determination and bold spirit. In President Lincoln's proclamation, he said, "I do therefore invite my fellow citizens in every part of the United States, and also those who are at sea and those who are sojourning in foreign lands, to set apart and observe the last Thursday of November next, as a day of Thanksgiving and Praise to our beneficent Father who dwelleth in the Heavens."

Each year, more and more attention is paid to the *way* we celebrate holidays rather than *why* we celebrate. I don't want to get so caught up in the decorating and cooking that I forget the true meaning.

It might be a good idea to read Lincoln's entire proclamation (you can quickly find it on Google) at your next Thanksgiving gathering so your children and grandchildren can know that there is much more behind this tradition than turkey and being out of school. It's about celebrating God's blessings and thanking Him for smiling down on us.

Working with Phil to get the meal ready for a Thanksgiving feast.

Cranberry & Cream Cheese Stacks

■ Makes 8 servings

8 ounces cream cheese, at room temperature

1 tablespoon maple syrup or honey

3 tablespoons finely chopped crystallized ginger (see Note)

½ cup finely chopped pecans, plus 8 pecan halves for garnish

2 teaspoons finely grated orange zest

2 cans (16 ounces each) jellied cranberry sauce

1. In a small bowl, stir together the cream cheese, maple syrup, crystallized ginger, chopped pecans, and orange zest.

2. Release the cranberry jelly from their cans and lay the jelly logs on their sides. Cut each log of cranberry sauce crosswise into 8 equal slices. Arrange 8 of the slices on a serving plate. Top each slice with about 2 tablespoons of the cream cheese mixture and use your fingertips to gently spread it to the edge of the slice. Top with the remaining slices to make a cranberry sauce sandwich. Garnish the top of each stack with a dollop of the cream cheese mixture and a pecan half.

3. Serve at room temperature or lightly chilled.

 *A Note from Miss Kay*

Look for bags of cubes or slices of soft crystallized ginger in the baking aisle or the candy aisle of your grocery store. Do not buy the "bakers' cut" ginger chips that come in a small can because the pieces are too hard to use in this recipe.

Turkey Gravy with Giblets

Makes about 3½ cups

Giblets (neck, gizzard, and heart)
   from 1 turkey
5 cups turkey or chicken broth,
   preferably homemade
1 cup diced onion
½ cup diced carrot
½ cup diced celery
1 bay leaf
1 teaspoon dried thyme
Pan drippings from roasting a turkey
   or turkey breast (see page 210)
2 to 4 tablespoons butter
¼ cup all-purpose flour
2 hard-cooked-eggs, finely chopped
   (optional, see Tip on page 75)
Salt and black pepper

1. Rinse the giblets and place in a large saucepan. Add the turkey broth, onion, carrot, celery, bay leaf, and thyme. Bring to a boil, reduce the heat, and simmer gently until the giblets are tender and the broth reduces to 3 cups, about 45 minutes. If the broth doesn't taste richly of turkey, continue simmering and reducing a little longer. Strain the broth into a large bowl and reserve the solids. Return the broth to the saucepan and keep warm over low heat.

2. Spoon off the fat from the top of the pan drippings (from roasting a turkey or turkey breast) and set aside the pan drippings in a small bowl. Pour the de-fatted drippings through a fine-mesh sieve into the broth.

3. When cool enough to handle, finely chop the gizzard and heart and place in a small bowl. Pull the meat from the neck and add to the bowl. Discard the neck bones and the other solids.

4. Measure out 4 tablespoons of reserved turkey fat into a large saucepan or skillet. If there is less than 4 tablespoons of fat, make up the difference with butter. If you have no turkey fat, use all butter. Heat over medium-high heat. Sprinkle the flour into the pan and whisk until smooth. Cook, whisking constantly, for 2 minutes.

5. Whisk in the warm turkey broth. Cook, stirring slowly and constantly, until the gravy thickens and comes just to a boil, about 10 minutes. Stir in the reserved giblets and neck meat. Stir in the hard-cooked eggs (if using). Season with salt and pepper to taste and serve hot.

A Note from Miss Kay

The giblets and neck come in a paper or plastic packet tucked inside the cavity of most whole turkeys, whether fresh or frozen. However, if you are roasting a turkey breast, there are no giblets. In that case, you can buy containers of turkey or chicken gizzards at most grocery stores, especially around the holidays. Another option is to use only turkey necks, which are also sold separately around the holidays. Not everyone enjoys the strong, distinctive taste of turkey liver in their giblet gravy, so don't use it if you don't like it. Even when you do want to use the liver, don't add it to the broth when you cook the other giblets because it can turn the broth bitter. Simmer the liver separately in a little salted water until tender, mash it with a fork, and stir it into the gravy right before serving.

Chrys and I attend a Thanksgiving feast with John Luke and Sadie.

Green Bean Casserole

■ *Makes 12 servings*

2 cans (10.75 ounces each) condensed cream of mushroom soup

1 cup whole milk

1 teaspoon soy sauce

1 teaspoon Worcestershire sauce

¼ teaspoon black pepper

8 cups cooked bite-size green beans, drained

1 can (2.8 ounces) crisp french-fried onions (I use French's), divided

1. Preheat the oven to 350°F.

2. In a large bowl, stir together the soup, milk, soy sauce, Worcestershire sauce, and pepper until smooth. Stir in the beans and half of the onions. Pour into a 9 x 13-inch baking dish.

3. Bake for 25 minutes. Sprinkle the remaining half of the onions over the top. Bake for 5 minutes more. Serve warm.

A Note from Miss Kay

Again, this is a tried-and-true dish taken to almost any event from family reunions to potlucks to Christmas dinner.

Candied Yams

Makes 4 to 6 servings

2 pounds small, slender yams (dark-skinned sweet potatoes)

½ teaspoon ground cinnamon

½ teaspoon ground nutmeg

1 stick (¼ pound) butter

½ cup packed dark brown sugar

¼ teaspoon salt, or to taste

A few sprigs of rosemary, chopped, for garnish (optional)

1. Peel the yams and cut them crosswise into 1½-inch rounds. Place in a large saucepan with cold water to cover. Add the cinnamon and nutmeg. Bring to a boil, reduce the heat, and cook at a low boil until tender when pierced with the tip of a knife, about 20 minutes. Do not let them get waterlogged. Drain well and return to the pan.

2. Add the butter and brown sugar. Cover the pan and let sit until the butter melts and then stir gently to coat. Season with the salt, sprinkle on rosemary, and serve warm.

Nothing says fall like Bella in a pumpkin patch.

A Note from Miss Kay

In Louisiana and other parts of the South, we sometimes use the word "yams" when we are talking about the tuber that other people call sweet potatoes.

Sweet Potato Biscuits

■ *Makes 1 dozen*

2 cups all-purpose flour

1 tablespoon baking powder

¼ teaspoon baking soda

1 teaspoon salt

2 tablespoons packed light brown sugar

1 stick (¼ pound) butter, cut into small cubes and chilled

¾ cup whole milk

1 cup baked (see Note) and mashed yam or sweet potato (about 1 medium), chilled

2 tablespoons butter, melted

1. Preheat the oven to 400°F. Line a rimmed baking sheet with parchment paper.

2. In a large bowl, whisk together the flour, baking powder, baking soda, salt, and brown sugar.

3. Work in the butter with a pastry blender or your fingertips until the mixture is crumbly with a few pieces of butter the size of green peas.

4. In a small bowl, whisk together the milk and mashed yam. Make a well in the center of the flour mixture, pour in the milk mixture, and stir to make a stiff dough.

5. Pour the dough onto a lightly floured surface. Roll with a floured pin to ¾-inch thickness. Using a 2½-inch round cutter, stamp out biscuits as close together as possible. Place the biscuits on the lined baking sheet. Gather and roll the scraps, and stamp out more biscuits.

6. Bake until firm and golden brown on the bottom, 12 to 15 minutes. Brush the tops with the melted butter and serve hot.

 *A Note from Miss Kay*

If you prefer to boil the sweet potato instead of baking it, leave it whole and unpeeled. If the cooked sweet potato flesh is stringy, use a rubber spatula to force it through a fine-mesh sieve into a bowl. The mashed sweet potato should have the consistency of canned pumpkin. If your sweet potato mash is too watery, put it back into the sieve, set it over a bowl to catch drips, and refrigerate for at least 4 hours and up to overnight. Discard the collected liquid.

Roasted Duck with Apple-Andouille Stuffing

■ *Makes 4 to 6 servings*

1 duck (4½ to 5 pounds)

Salt and black pepper

2 tablespoons butter

1 small onion, chopped (about 1 cup)

1 celery stalk, chopped (about ½ cup)

1 green apple, cored and cut into small dice (about 1½ cups)

6 ounces andouille sausage, halved lengthwise and cut crosswise into ¼-inch slices

3 cups crumbled cornbread

¼ cup chopped pecans

¼ cup golden raisins

1 tablespoon chopped fresh sage

¼ cup finely chopped flat-leaf parsley

½ cup chicken broth

1 large egg, beaten

1. Preheat the oven to 375°F. Line a rimmed baking sheet with foil. Set a wire rack inside the baking sheet.

2. Season the duck inside and out with salt and pepper. Place the duck breast side up on the wire rack.

3. Melt the butter in a large skillet over medium-high heat. Add the onion, celery, and apple and cook, stirring occasionally, until tender, about 5 minutes. Pour into a large bowl.

4. Stir in the andouille, cornbread, pecans, raisins, sage, and parsley. Stir in the broth. Stir in the egg.

5. Spoon some stuffing into the duck cavity, packing it loosely. Tuck a sheet of foil around the end of the duck to cover the stuffing so that it won't burn. Spoon the remaining stuffing into a buttered small baking dish and refrigerate until needed.

6. Roast the duck until an instant-read thermometer inserted into the thickest part of a thigh without touching bone registers 180°F, 2½ to 3 hours. For even browning and the crispest skin, rotate pan every 30 minutes.

7. Add the baking dish of stuffing to the oven during the last 20 to 30 minutes of roasting time. Let the duck rest for 10 minutes before serving.

Tip: Keep an eye on the duck as it cooks to ensure that the fat doesn't overflow the edges of the pan. But don't be tempted to use a deep roasting pan, or the sides of the duck won't brown.

A Note from Miss Kay

As you might suspect, we love duck! And duck and sausage is the best! Your family will thank you for serving this fabulous recipe.

Herb-Roasted Turkey Breast

■ *Makes 6 to 8 servings*

1 bone-in turkey breast (about
    6 pounds)
2 tablespoons butter, at room
    temperature
1 tablespoon lemon juice
2 teaspoons salt, plus more as needed
1 teaspoon black pepper
1 teaspoon dried thyme
1 teaspoon dried sage
1 teaspoon dried rosemary
1 large onion, peeled and cut into
    wedges
2 celery stalks, coarsely chopped
1 large carrot, coarsely chopped
2 tablespoons butter, melted
2 cups turkey or chicken broth

 *A Note from Miss Kay*

Roasting the turkey on a shallow rimmed baking sheet instead of a deep roasting pan helps it brown evenly on the sides. It might be more traditional to roast a whole turkey, but turkey breasts are easier to handle and cook in much less time. Even if you still want to prepare a whole turkey to place in the center of the table, consider roasting one or two turkey breasts so that you'll have plenty of white meat to serve all your guests, not to mention plenty of leftovers for sandwiches, soups, and casseroles.

1. Remove the turkey from the refrigerator 30 minutes before roasting. Preheat the oven to 450°F.

2. In a small bowl, stir together the room temperature butter, the lemon juice, salt, pepper, thyme, sage, and rosemary. Gently loosen the skin on the top of the turkey, taking care to not rip holes in the skin. Place the butter mixture under the skin, replace the skin, and massage gently to spread the butter as evenly as possible under the skin.

3. Generously season the turkey cavity with salt and pepper. Place the turkey on a wire rack set inside a rimmed baking sheet. Place the onion, celery, and carrot inside the turkey cavity. Brush the top of the turkey with the melted butter.

4. Place the turkey in the oven. Carefully pour about 1 cup broth into the baking sheet. Do not let the pan cook dry while the turkey roasts; add more broth as needed. (This creates the delicious pan drippings that you can use in the gravy or drizzle over the carved turkey.)

5. Roast the turkey for 30 minutes. Reduce the oven temperature to 350°F and continue roasting until an instant-read thermometer inserted into the thickest part of the meat without touching bone registers 165°F. Check the temperature on both sides of the breast to make sure. Tent the turkey loosely with foil if the skin on top browns too quickly.

6. Let the turkey rest at room temperature for 15 minutes before carving. Drizzle with the pan juices if you are not using them to make turkey gravy.

Pan-Fried Quail with Gravy

■ *Makes 4 to 8 servings*

Quail

2 cups buttermilk

1 tablespoon Worcestershire sauce

½ teaspoon hot sauce

8 semi-boneless quail (4 to 5 ounces each)

1 cup all-purpose flour

2 teaspoons onion powder

2 teaspoons garlic powder

1 teaspoon paprika

2 teaspoons Cajun seasoning blend

1 teaspoon salt

½ teaspoon black pepper

3 tablespoons butter

3 tablespoons vegetable oil

Gravy

3 tablespoons reserved seasoned flour from quail

2½ cups chicken broth, warmed

½ cup half-and-half, warmed

Kosher salt and black pepper

1. For the quail: Pour the buttermilk, Worcestershire sauce, and hot sauce into a large zip-top freezer bag. Add the quail, squeeze out excess air, close the bag tightly, and refrigerate for 2 hours. Turn the bag over once in a while to make sure the quail is covered evenly.

2. In a shallow bowl, whisk together the flour, onion powder, garlic powder, paprika, Cajun seasoning, salt, and pepper.

3. Working with one quail at a time, remove from the buttermilk and let excess drip off. Lightly and evenly coat the quail in the flour mixture. Set aside in a single layer until all the quail are coated. Set aside 3 tablespoons of the flour mixture to use in the gravy (discard the rest).

4. In a large cast-iron skillet, melt the butter and oil over medium-high heat. Working in batches of 2 or 3 quail at a time, place them in the hot oil. Fry undisturbed until well browned on the bottom, 4 to 6 minutes. Turn with tongs and brown the other side, 4 to 6 minutes more. Adjust the heat if the coating darkens too quickly. When done, an instant-read thermometer inserted into thickest part of the meat without touching bone should register 165°F. Transfer the cooked quail to a large plate and tent loosely with foil to keep warm.

5. For the gravy: Pour off all but 3 tablespoons fat from the skillet, taking care not to dislodge any browned bits on the bottom of the skillet. Sprinkle the 3 tablespoons reserved seasoned flour into the skillet and whisk until smooth. Cook, whisking constantly, for 2 minutes. Whisk in the warm

broth. Cook, stirring constantly with a spatula, until the gravy thickens and comes just to a boil, about 5 minutes. Stir in the half-and-half and heat through. Check the seasoning and add salt and pepper as needed.

6. Serve the warm quail with the hot gravy.

 *A Note from Miss Kay*

It might sound strange to you, but quail can be bought at many grocery stores. So if you're up for something a little different, I think you'll like this recipe.

Oyster Dressing

▮ Makes 12 servings

Cooking spray
½ stick (4 tablespoons) butter, melted
2 cups chopped onion
1 cup chopped celery
2 cups diced red bell pepper
2 cups diced green bell pepper
1 pint freshly shucked oysters with their liquor, drained, liquor reserved
¼ cup chopped green onions (scallions)
4 cups cubed (1-inch) sturdy bread
2 cups crumbled cornbread
¼ cup finely chopped flat-leaf parsley
1 tablespoon fresh thyme leaves
½ teaspoon salt
1 teaspoon black pepper
1 to 3 cups chicken broth
2 large eggs, beaten
⅓ cup finely grated Parmesan cheese

1. Preheat the oven to 375°F. Mist a 9 x 13-inch baking dish with cooking spray.

2. In a large pot, melt the butter over medium-high heat. Add the onion, celery, red bell pepper, and green bell pepper and cook, stirring often, until tender, about 5 minutes.

3. Add the oysters and cook, stirring, until the edges begin to curl, about 2 minutes. Pour into a very large bowl. Stir in the green onions.

4. Add the bread cubes, cornbread, parsley, thyme, salt, and pepper and mix well.

5. If you like a strong oyster flavor, add some or all of the reserved liquor, keeping in mind that a little goes a long way. Add enough broth to make the dressing moist and mix well. Stir in the eggs.

6. Spoon into the baking dish, sprinkle with the Parmesan, and bake until lightly browned, about 45 minutes. Serve warm.

 *A Note from Miss Kay*

Most people carry a lifelong preference for the type of dressing that their families ate while growing up. In Louisiana and much of the South, many love oyster dressing.

Dirty Rice

Makes 6 to 8 servings

2 slices bacon, chopped

1 cup chopped onion

½ cup chopped green bell pepper

¼ cup chopped celery

2 garlic cloves, chopped

1 jalapeño pepper, seeded and finely chopped

4 ounces cleaned chicken and/or duck livers, very finely chopped or pureed (about ½ cup)

4 ounces lean ground pork or beef

4 cups cooked and cooled long-grain white rice

½ teaspoon salt

¼ teaspoon black pepper

2 teaspoons Creole seasoning blend, such as Tony Chachere's

¼ cup chopped green onions (scallions)

¼ cup chopped flat-leaf parsley

Hot sauce, to taste

1. Cook the bacon in a large skillet over medium-high heat until crisp, stirring often, about 10 minutes. Move to a small bowl with a slotted spoon, leaving the drippings in the skillet.

2. Add the onion, bell pepper, and celery to the skillet and cook, stirring often, until tender, about 5 minutes. Add the garlic and jalapeño and cook 1 minute.

3. Add the pureed liver and ground pork and cook, stirring often, until the pork is no longer pink.

4. Stir in the rice, salt, black pepper, and Creole seasoning. Cook, stirring occasionally, until heated through, 15 to 20 minutes.

5. Stir in the reserved bacon, green onions, and parsley. Season with the hot sauce. Check the seasoning and serve warm.

 *A Note from Miss Kay*

Rice is a staple in Louisiana, and Dirty Rice is a favorite. You can serve this with anything Southern!

Pumpkin Pie with Brown Sugar Whipped Cream

■ *Makes 8 servings*

Pie

One 9-inch deep-dish piecrust, store-bought or homemade (see Note)
1 can (15 ounces) pumpkin puree
1 cup half-and-half
3 large eggs
½ cup packed light brown sugar
¼ cup sugar
1 tablespoon cornstarch
1 teaspoon ground cinnamon
½ teaspoon ground ginger
⅛ teaspoon ground cloves
¼ teaspoon ground allspice
¼ teaspoon ground nutmeg

Whipped Cream

1 cup whipping cream, chilled
¼ cup powdered sugar
2 tablespoons packed light brown sugar
½ teaspoon vanilla extract
¼ teaspoon maple flavoring (optional)

 *A Note from Miss Kay*

If you'd like to make your own piecrust, follow the recipe on page 118, but roll the crust out round instead of rectangular. That recipe will make enough for two pie shells, but you can freeze the dough for the second crust to use later.

1. For the pie: If using a store-bought piecrust, follow the package directions for baking an unfilled crust. Leave the oven on but increase the temperature to 375°F. Let the piecrust cool on a wire rack for 15 minutes. If using a homemade piecrust, see page 78 for directions.

2. In a large bowl, whisk together the pumpkin puree, half-and-half, and eggs until well blended. Whisk in the brown sugar, sugar, cornstarch, cinnamon, ginger, cloves, allspice, and nutmeg. Pour into the crust.

3. Bake until the tip of a sharp knife inserted into the center comes out clean, 50 to 55 minutes. Shield the edge of the crust with foil if it browns too quickly. Cool to room temperature on a wire rack. Cover and refrigerate until chilled before serving, at least 4 hours and preferably overnight.

4. For the whipped cream: Pour the chilled cream into a medium chilled bowl. Beat with the chilled beaters of an electric mixer until the cream begins to thicken. Add the powdered sugar, brown sugar, vanilla, and maple flavoring (if using). Beat the cream to stiff peaks.

6. Serve the pie topped with a big dollop of the whipped cream.

Chocolate Sheet Cake

Makes 20 to 24 servings

Cake

2 cups all-purpose flour
2 cups sugar
1 teaspoon baking soda
¼ teaspoon salt
2 sticks (½ pound) butter
⅓ cup unsweetened cocoa powder
1 cup water
2 large eggs
½ cup buttermilk
1½ teaspoons vanilla extract

Chocolate Pecan Frosting

½ stick (4 tablespoons) butter
3 tablespoons unsweetened cocoa powder
¼ cup buttermilk
2¼ cups sifted powdered sugar
½ teaspoon vanilla extract
½ cup chopped pecans

1. For the cake: Preheat the oven to 350°F. Grease and flour a 10 x 15-inch or 9 x 13-inch baking pan (see Note).

2. In a large bowl, with an electric mixer, whisk together the flour, sugar, baking soda, and salt.

3. In a medium saucepan, combine the butter, cocoa powder, and water and bring to a boil over high heat, stirring constantly.

4. Pour the hot butter mixture into the flour mixture and beat on medium speed until well blended. Add the eggs, buttermilk, and vanilla and beat for 1 minute. The batter will be thin. Pour into the baking pan.

5. Bake until a wooden pick inserted into the center comes out clean, 20 to 25 minutes for a 10 x 15-inch cake, or 30 to 35 minutes for a 9 x 13-inch cake. Set aside on a wire rack while you make the frosting.

6. For the frosting: In a medium saucepan, combine the butter, cocoa powder, and buttermilk. Stir over high heat until the mixture boils. Remove from the heat and stir in the powdered sugar and vanilla. Beat with an electric mixer on medium speed until smooth. Stir in the pecans.

7. Pour the warm frosting over the warm cake, spreading evenly. Let the cake cool to room temperature on a wire rack before cutting.

 *A Note from Miss Kay*

It's unusual to give a choice of pan sizes for a cake, but this one works equally well in either size, although they yield different results. The larger pan yields thin squares of cake that resemble a brownie. The smaller pan yields deeper, fluffier pieces that are more like traditional cake.

- *12* -

Christmas

Celebrated on the Twenty-Fifth Day of December

■ ■ ■ ■ ■

Christmas, my child, is love in action.
Every time we love, every time we give, it's Christmas.
—DALE EVANS

He will be a joy and a delight to you,

and many will rejoice because of his birth.

—LUKE 1:14 NIV

Recipes for Christmas Day

Does it get any better than this? Christmas morning with one of my boys.

Celebrating the Birth of Jesus

Christmas is definitely my favorite holiday! My philosophy is you can never have too many Christmas recipes or decorations. I love to decorate nearly every inch of my house! And I love Christmas music, twinkling lights, buying fun presents, and of course, cooking delicious meals for my family. I love it all!

When I was a little girl, I was chosen for the lead role in the Christmas play, which was performed in front of the whole church. I remember being so surprised I was chosen, and to this day, don't know why they picked me. Maybe the lady in charge knew how much I loved Christmas and knew I would love being in the play. That experience opened my eyes to the value of empowering children in all areas of life. I've taught Sunday school classes for years, and I love to see my grown "children" read from the Bible and lead singing in church services.

Another precious memory I have of Christmas past is going to my grandmother's house. Normally, her house was always cold—as they didn't heat the rooms that were not used—but at Christmas, she would heat her living room and let me sit for hours looking at the lights on the tree. Compared to today's decorations, I'm sure

I've always loved Christmas!

it wasn't much, but to me, it was magical. I'm sure that's why I still get my boys to light up my entire house!

Of all the holidays, Christmas is the one that either gets you fired up or wears you out—and maybe both. There can be church events to go to, school parties to buy for, work parties to organize, gifts to pick up for family and friends, a house to decorate and, if you're really on top of it, cards to send out. Whew! No wonder people get exhausted at Christmas.

I'll give you a tip that will make your "holiday" life easier. The Bible tells us to be "agreeable as much as it depends on you." In other words, there are some people you will never make happy, but as much as it depends on you, help keep the peace. I learned a long time ago that any holiday goes more smoothly if everyone does his or her best to be accommodating. With four sons, I knew I would need to work around the holiday plans of their wives, so I made sure all my daughters-in-law knew that our family would celebrate whenever it worked for everyone else. So far, we've been able to work out scheduling for every holiday without hurt feelings and regrets. That's quite an accomplishment with a family as large as ours.

Jesus's birth, life, and death are about love. After all, He is the prince of peace. It would not honor Him in any way if the day we celebrate His birth was filled with strife. The birth of Jesus is recorded in all four gospels: Matthew, Mark, Luke, and John, and each account gives us insight into who Jesus is and what He did. It's common knowledge that we don't know exactly on which day Jesus was born. In fact, many scholars believe he was born in the spring, which would be more likely since the weather would be warm and the people could travel to the required annual census more comfortably. But knowing the exact date isn't important; knowing who Jesus was and what He did is.

Christmas is about giving gifts, but there's no greater gift than the one Jesus gave in His coming, His death, and His resurrection. Jesus walked among us so He could understand us and relate to us. In exchange, He simply asks us to walk with Him. As you celebrate Jesus's birth this year, give yourself a gift. Get to know Jesus by reading about Him, praying to Him, and worshipping Him. He doesn't need it, but He does deserve it. Merry Christmas!

Festive Holiday Cheese Ball

■ *Makes 12 servings*

2 packages (8 ounces each) cream cheese, at room temperature

2 teaspoons Worcestershire sauce

1 teaspoon garlic powder

1 teaspoon hot sauce, or to taste

1 teaspoon lemon juice

8 ounces extra-sharp cheddar cheese, grated (about 2 cups)

2 tablespoons finely chopped green onions (scallions)

2 tablespoons finely chopped red bell pepper

2 cups salted or smoked whole almonds

1 or 2 short, full sprigs fresh rosemary, for garnish

Good crackers, for serving

1. In a large bowl, stir together the cream cheese, Worcestershire sauce, garlic powder, hot sauce, and lemon juice until smooth. Stir in the cheese, green onions, and bell pepper.

2. Scrape the mixture onto a large sheet of plastic wrap. Form into a tapered triangle with rounded corners to resemble a pine cone. Starting at the tapered end, arrange the almonds in parallel rows over the top and side of the cheese mixture, slightly overlapping the points and positioning them to look like the scales of a pine cone. Wrap in the plastic wrap and refrigerate until firm.

3. Let sit at room temperature for 20 minutes before serving. Just before serving, insert the rosemary in the top to look like greenery. Serve with crackers.

A Note from Miss Kay

If you don't want to decorate the cheese ball so elaborately, it tastes just as good when formed into a ball and rolled in chopped almonds.

Even though I'm not a skier, a family ski trip is a great way to spend Christmas together.

Ambrosia

Makes 6 servings

1 cup sour cream

½ teaspoon ground ginger

2 tablespoons sugar

1 can (11 ounces) mandarin oranges, drained

1 can (8 ounces) pineapple chunks, drained

½ cup sweetened flaked coconut

½ cup chopped pecans

1 cup mini marshmallows (optional)

Maraschino cherries with stems, for garnish

1. In a large serving bowl, stir together the sour cream, ginger, and sugar.

2. Add the oranges, pineapple, coconut, pecans, and marshmallows (if using) and stir gently to coat.

3. Cover and refrigerate until chilled, at least 2 hours. Serve garnished with cherries.

Sadie and her cousins from Korie's side of the family show off their skills.

 *A Note from Miss Kay*

This is an old Southern recipe, but a good one. It's pretty and delicious.

Sausage & Potato Breakfast Casserole

Makes 16 servings

Cooking spray
1 pound bulk pork breakfast sausage
1 large onion, chopped (about 3 cups)
1 bag (32 ounces) frozen hash browns, thawed
3 cups (12 ounces) shredded sharp cheddar cheese, divided
6 large eggs
2 cups whole milk
1 teaspoon mustard powder
1 teaspoon paprika
1 teaspoon salt
½ teaspoon black pepper
Salsa, for serving (optional)

1. Preheat the oven to 350°F. Mist a 9 x 13-inch baking dish with cooking spray.

2. In a large skillet, cook the sausage over medium-high heat until no longer pink, about 5 minutes. Add the onion and cook, stirring often, until the sausage is browned and the onion is tender, about 5 minutes. Remove from the heat.

3. Spread half of the hash browns in the bottom of the baking dish. Top with half the cheese. Use a slotted spoon to transfer the sausage mixture to the dish (leaving any liquid in the skillet) and sprinkle it evenly over the cheese. Top with the remaining hash browns, followed by the remaining cheese.

4. In a medium bowl, whisk together the eggs, milk, mustard powder, paprika, salt, and pepper. Pour evenly over the potato mixture.

5. Cover the dish with foil and bake until a knife inserted into the center comes out clean, about 40 minutes. Let stand for 10 minutes before cutting. Serve with salsa if desired.

 *A Note from Miss Kay*

This casserole is tasty on its own, but some of my boys like this casserole served with salsa. Either way, it's delicious!

Crescent Roll Wreath Appetizer

Makes 8 to 12 servings

Cooking spray

8 ounces chive and onion cream
cheese, at room temperature

1 cup finely chopped fresh or thawed
frozen broccoli florets

½ cup finely chopped red bell pepper

¼ cup finely chopped water chestnuts

2 tablespoons finely chopped green
onions (scallions)

¼ cup finely chopped baked ham or
crisp-cooked bacon (optional)

Salt and black pepper

2 cans (8 ounces each) refrigerated
crescent roll dough

1 large egg

1 tablespoon cold water

2 teaspoons sesame seeds

1. Preheat the oven to 375°F. Mist a 12- to 14-inch pizza pan with cooking spray.

2. In a medium bowl, stir together the cream cheese, broccoli, bell pepper, water chestnuts, green onions, and ham (if using). Season with salt and pepper to taste.

3. Unwrap the crescent roll dough and separate along the perforations into 16 triangles. Arrange the triangles in a circle with the wide sides toward the center and the long, tapered points facing out over the edge of the pan; leave a 5-inch-wide open space in the center. Let the edges of the wide sides overlap slightly and gently press them together.

4. Spoon the cream cheese mixture onto the widest part of the circle of dough. Pull the long points of dough over the filling and tuck under the ends to form a ring. Some of the filling will remain visible between the strips of dough. The finished round should resemble a wreath.

5. Whisk together the egg and water. Brush the dough with the egg mixture and sprinkle with the sesame seeds. Bake until the dough is deep golden brown, 20 to 25 minutes. Cool on the pan for 5 minutes. Run a metal spatula under the wreath and then slide it onto a serving platter. Slice and serve warm or at room temperature.

 *A Note from Miss Kay*

This one takes a little effort, but it's worth it! With this wreath, you get both good food and a pretty decoration. You can add a pretty Christmas ribbon (see photo) for an extra special look.

Crab Spread

Makes 12 to 16 servings

2 tablespoons butter

2 green onions (scallions), finely chopped (about 2 tablespoons)

¼ cup finely chopped red bell pepper

8 ounces cream cheese

1 tablespoons mayonnaise

1 tablespoon Dijon mustard

1 teaspoon Worcestershire sauce

½ teaspoon salt, or to taste

¼ teaspoon black pepper, or to taste

1 teaspoon hot sauce, or to taste

2 teaspoons Old Bay seasoning, plus more for sprinkling

2 tablespoons finely chopped flat-leaf parsley

12 ounces lump crabmeat, picked through for bits of shell

1 to 4 tablespoons heavy cream, as needed

Toasted baguette slices or good crackers, for serving

1. In a large saucepan, melt the butter over medium-high heat. Add the green onions and bell pepper and cook, stirring often, until tender, about 5 minutes.

2. Add the cream cheese, mayonnaise, mustard, Worcestershire sauce, salt, pepper, hot sauce, Old Bay, and parsley and mix well. Cook over medium-low heat until heated through.

3. Fold in the crabmeat. If the mixture is too thick, stir in heavy cream as needed. Season with more salt and pepper to taste.

4. Sprinkle with Old Bay and serve warm with baguette slices or crackers.

 *A Note from Miss Kay*

A small slow cooker is a nice way to keep this warm during a party. Be sure to buy chilled crab from the seafood department in your store. It is usually packaged in plastic containers. Canned crab on the grocery aisle isn't a good choice for this recipe.

Scalloped Potatoes

Makes 12 servings

2 cups heavy cream

2 cups whole milk

4 garlic cloves, thinly sliced

2 tablespoons fresh thyme leaves

1 bay leaf

¼ teaspoon grated nutmeg

2 teaspoons salt

½ teaspoon black pepper

4 pounds Yukon Gold potatoes

2 tablespoons butter, cut into small
  cubes

1. Preheat the oven to 350°F. Generously butter a shallow 2½-quart baking dish.

2. In a large saucepan, stir together the cream, milk, garlic, thyme, bay leaf, nutmeg, salt, and pepper.

3. Working with one potato at a time, peel the potatoes and cut into ⅛-inch slices. Put the slices immediately into the cream mixture to keep them from turning dark. When all of the potatoes are in the pan, bring just to a simmer over medium-high heat. Using a slotted spoon, move the potatoes to the baking dish, spreading them evenly. Pour the cream mixture over the potatoes.

4. Dot the top with butter. Bake until golden brown and bubbling, about 40 minutes. Let sit 15 minutes before serving warm.

 *A Note from Miss Kay*

A vegetable slicer makes quick work of slicing the potatoes, but you can also use a knife. Either way, it's important that the slices have a uniform thickness so that they cook evenly.

Pickled Shrimp

■ Makes 6 to 8 servings

1 pound medium (26/30 count) cooked shrimp, peeled and deveined (leave the tails on)

1 medium red onion, halved and thinly sliced

1 lemon, thinly sliced

¾ cup white wine vinegar

½ cup extra-virgin olive oil

¼ cup drained capers

½ teaspoon celery seeds

1 teaspoon sugar

½ teaspoon salt

¼ teaspoon red pepper flakes, or to taste

¼ cup chopped flat-leaf parsley

1. Arrange half of the shrimp in a large glass serving bowl, such as a trifle bowl. Top with half of the onion and half the lemon. Repeat the layers.

2. In a medium bowl, stir together the vinegar, oil, capers, celery seeds, sugar, salt, and pepper flakes. Pour over the shrimp, letting it trickle down over the layers. Cover and refrigerate overnight.

3. Just before serving, stir gently and sprinkle the parsley on top.

 *A Note from Miss Kay*

The best thing about this dish is that it can be done the night before. Any holiday brings added pressure, so take some pressure off and look for recipes that can be done ahead of time.

Roasted Pork Loin

Makes 8 servings

3 tablespoons grainy Dijon mustard

1 pork loin roast (2½ to 3 pounds), trimmed and tied

8 garlic cloves, chopped

4 teaspoons chopped fresh rosemary

1 tablespoon salt

1 teaspoon black pepper

1. Preheat the oven to 375°F. Line a rimmed baking sheet with foil. Set a wire rack inside the pan.

2. Rub the mustard all over the roast. In a small bowl, stir together the garlic, rosemary, salt, and pepper and sprinkle over the mustard. Place the roast on the wire rack.

3. Roast until an instant-read thermometer inserted horizontally into the end of the roast registers 145°F, about 35 minutes. Transfer to a cutting board and let rest for 10 minutes before removing the string and slicing. The internal temperature will increase about another 5°F as it rests.

4. Slice and serve drizzled with any pan juices.

 *A Note from Miss Kay*

Be sure to buy a pork loin, not a pork tenderloin, which is much smaller. Our family is very large, so two loin roasts are often needed.

Broccoli & Rice Casserole

Makes 12 servings

Cooking spray

2 tablespoons butter

1 cup finely chopped celery

1 cup finely chopped onion

1 can (10.75 ounces) condensed cream of mushroom soup

1 can (10.75 ounces) condensed cream of celery soup

1 can (12 ounces) evaporated milk

1 loaf (16 ounces) Velveeta, cut into 1-inch cubes

1 teaspoon salt

½ teaspoon black pepper

4 cups cooked and cooled chopped broccoli

3 cups cooked and cooled long-grain white rice

1. Preheat the oven to 350°F. Mist a 9 x 13-inch baking dish with cooking spray.

2. In a large saucepan, melt the butter over medium-high heat. Add the celery and onion and cook, stirring occasionally, until tender, about 5 minutes.

3. Stir in the cream of mushroom soup, cream of celery soup, and evaporated milk and stir until well mixed. Bring to a simmer, add the Velveeta, and cook, stirring constantly, until melted and smooth. Stir in the salt, pepper, broccoli, and rice.

4. Pour into the baking dish and bake until golden brown and bubbling, about 45 minutes. Let stand 10 minutes before serving warm.

 *A Note from Miss Kay*

This is a favorite at any event I go to. I have it in my Christmas chapter, but it's perfect for any occasion.

Foolproof Beef Tenderloin with Creamy Horseradish Sauce

 Makes 8 to 10 servings

 Beef

1 beef tenderloin (4 to 5 pounds), trimmed and tied
3 tablespoons vegetable oil
4 teaspoons coarse or kosher salt
3 teaspoons cracked or coarsely ground black pepper

Sauce

1 cup whipping cream, chilled
1 cup sour cream
1 teaspoon salt
2 to 4 tablespoons bottled horseradish
1 tablespoon green peppercorns, drained
1 tablespoon chopped chives

1. For the beef: Remove the beef from the refrigerator 1 hour before roasting.

2. Preheat the oven to 275°F. Line a rimmed baking sheet with foil. Set a wire rack inside the pan.

3. Pat the beef dry with paper towels and then rub lightly and evenly with the oil. Sprinkle with the salt and pepper. Place on the rack. Roast until an instant-read thermometer inserted horizontally into the end of the tenderloin registers 130° to 135°F for medium-rare or 135° to 140°F for medium, for 1 hour to 1 hour 15 minutes. Let rest 20 minutes before carving. The internal temperature will continue to rise about 5°F as the beef rests.

4. For the sauce: In a large chilled bowl, with the chilled beaters of an electric mixer on high speed, whip the cream to stiff peaks. Fold in the sour cream, salt, horseradish, and peppercorns. Cover and refrigerate until needed. Just before serving, sprinkle with the chives.

5. Remove the strings from the beef and cut into thick slices. Serve with the sauce.

 *A Note from Miss Kay*

Some grocery stores trim the excess fat from tenderloins and tie them with butcher string before putting them in the meat case. If not, you can ask your butcher to do this for you. Tying the roast helps it hold its shape while it roasts, which makes it cook evenly. Beef tenderloins are expensive and often made only on special occasions, so you want it to turn out right. Rely on an instant-read thermometer to tell you when it's done.

Holiday Punch

■ *Makes about 4 quarts*

3 cups pomegranate juice, chilled

3 cups cranberry juice cocktail, chilled

6 cups pineapple juice, chilled

4 cups lemon-lime soft drink

Pomegranate seeds, frozen cranberries, and small mint sprigs, for garnish

1. In a large pitcher or punch bowl, stir together the pomegranate juice, cranberry juice cocktail, and pineapple juice. Just before serving, stir in the soft drink. Serve soon, before the soft drink loses its fizz.

2. Place a few pomegranate seeds and cranberries in the bottom of the serving glasses before pouring in the punch. Top each serving with mint.

A Note from Miss Kay

To make the punch a little less sweet, use seltzer or sparkling water in place of the soft drink.
This is pretty served in tall champagne flutes.

Bella loves Christmas cookie decorating!

Chocolate Pecan Fudge

Makes 4 dozen squares

3 cups sugar
1½ sticks (12 tablespoons) butter
⅔ cup evaporated milk
12 ounces semisweet chocolate chips
1 jar (7 ounces) marshmallow crème
1 teaspoon vanilla extract
1 cup chopped pecans

1. Line a 9 x 13-inch baking dish with a long sheet of foil, leaving overhang on two ends to use as handles to remove the fudge.

2. In a large saucepan, combine the sugar, butter, and milk and bring to a full, rolling boil over medium heat. Boil, stirring constantly, until the mixture reaches 235°F (soft ball stage) on a candy thermometer, about 5 minutes.

3. Remove from the heat, add the chocolate chips, and stir until melted and smooth. Beat in the marshmallow crème and vanilla with a wooden spoon. Stir in the pecans.

4. Spread the fudge into the lined baking dish and let cool to room temperature. Fold the foil to form handles and lift out the fudge. Remove the foil and cut the fudge into squares.

 *A Note from Miss Kay*

Making fudge (or any kind of candy) can be intimidating. It's true that everything has to be done quickly, but it's fun to make and delicious to eat—especially at holiday time. If you've never made fudge before, give this recipe a try. You'll be surprised at how simple it is.

Easy Cinnamon Rolls

 Makes 1 dozen

Rolls

1 bag frozen dinner roll dough, such as Rhodes (for 12 rolls)
1 stick (¼ pound) butter, melted
½ cup sugar
2 teaspoons ground cinnamon
Cooking spray
⅓ cup heavy cream

Icing

¾ cup powdered sugar, sifted
1 tablespoon whole milk, plus more if needed
½ teaspoon vanilla extract

1. For the rolls: Thaw the dough and let rise according to the package directions.

2. Place the melted butter in a shallow dish. In a second shallow dish, stir together the sugar and cinnamon.

3. Separate the rolls. Working with one roll at a time, use your hands to stretch and pull the dough into a rope that is about 6 inches long. Dip the rope into the melted butter and then lightly and evenly coat in the cinnamon sugar. Spiral the dough into a coil and place in a 7 x 11-inch baking dish. Repeat for all 12 pieces of dough. Sprinkle any remaining cinnamon sugar over the tops. Mist a sheet of plastic wrap with cooking spray and cover the rolls. Follow the package directions for letting the dough rise a second time; the coils will double in size and be nested snugly in the pan, which helps them hold their shape.

4. Preheat the oven to 350°F.

5. Uncover the rolls and drizzle the heavy cream over them. Bake until golden brown, about 20 minutes.

6. For the icing: In a small bowl, whisk together the powdered sugar, milk, and vanilla until smooth. The icing should pour off a spoon easily, so add a little more milk, if needed.

7. Drizzle the icing over the warm cinnamon rolls and serve at once.

 *A Note from Miss Kay*

There's nothing better than the smell of cinnamon rolls in the oven, but homemade does take time. Try this "nearly" homemade recipe—the same great smell, but not as time consuming.

Red Velvet Cake

■ *Makes 16 servings*

Cake

1 box red velvet cake mix
Ingredients listed on cake mix
   package for preparing batter

Cream Cheese Frosting

4 packages (8 ounces each) cream
   cheese, at room temperature (do
   not use reduced-fat or nonfat)
2 sticks (½ pound) unsalted butter, at
   room temperature
1 teaspoon vanilla extract
1 tablespoon lemon juice
2 boxes (1 pound each) powdered
   sugar
1 to 2 cups pecan halves, for garnish

1. For the cake: Prepare the cake batter according
   to the package directions to make three 8-inch or
   two 9-inch layers. Bake as directed and cool the
   cake layers to room temperature before frosting.

2. For the frosting: In a large bowl, with an electric
   mixer at high speed, beat the cream cheese
   and butter until well blended and fluffy, about
   2 minutes. Beat in the vanilla and lemon juice.

3. Beat in the powdered sugar 2 cups at a time,
   beating until the frosting is light and fluffy and
   holds its shape when the beaters are lifted. Use at
   once.

4. To assemble the cake, spread about 1¼ cups of
   frosting between the layers as you stack them on
   a cake plate. Cover the top and sides of cake with a
   very thin layer of frosting. This thin layer is called
   a crumb coat and helps prevent cake crumbs from
   mixing into the final layer of frosting. Refrigerate
   for 20 minutes.

5. Frost the cake with as much of the remaining
   frosting as you like, making pretty swirls with the
   back of a spoon. Decorate the top and sides of the
   cake with pecans. Refrigerate for 30 minutes or
   until the frosting sets.

 A Note from Miss Kay

*Vegetable shortening, such as Crisco, works best to grease cake pans. Make sure the pans are covered
lightly and evenly. Dust generously with all-purpose flour, then turn the pans over and tap to
remove any excess. This recipe makes a lot of frosting. You will have plenty for the cake. If you have
leftover icing, you can use it for another recipe. This recipe does fine with a cake mix. We're all busy
these days, so don't feel guilty about using a mix. Just make homemade cream cheese frosting, and
everyone will love it!*

Thank-Yous

Chrys Howard: We get to share a lot of great moments, but the moments spent sharing grandchildren with you are my favorite. We have watched them grow from babies to engaged young adults and now to appearing on popular TV shows, playing football, and cheering. We've been able to watch Rebecca grow from a teenager who could barely speak English to a college graduate and flourish in her job as part owner of Duck & Dressing boutique. Each one brings us such joy and I am happy, happy, happy to share that with you. Sharing grandbabies is the best! I never dreamed I would do one cookbook, let alone two! Thank you for helping bring both cookbooks to life.

Jenny Remsberg: You are such an example to my Muffin groups, speaking and helping with whatever I need you to do. You were a great help to me during the photo shoot and the process of putting this cookbook together. I am so grateful God placed you in my life and blessed me with your friendship. Thank you for the time, effort, and energy you put into making this book great.

Food stylists and photo team: I can make food taste good, but you guys make it look good!!! And you make me look good, too!! Jennifer, Missy, Marion, and Emily—you're simply the *best*!

Index

Permissions and Photograph Credits

The Duck Commander logo is a trademark of Duck Commander, Inc.

Photographs

Courtesy of the Robertson family and Chrys Howard: v, 7, 16, 20, 26, 28, 37, 38, 46, 50, 59, 64, 66, 70, 74, 79, 86, 93, 96, 105, 107, 124, 126, 130, 144, 145, 146, 155, 164, 165, 169, 180, 182, 188, 194, 195, 202, 205, 207, 222, 223, 225, 226, 237

© Photography by Jennifer Davick: x, xiv, 10, 15, 19, 22, 31, 34, 39, 40, 49, 52, 57, 60, 69, 73, 77, 80, 89, 92, 97, 100, 108, 113, 114, 117, 120, 128, 133, 136, 139, 140, 148, 153, 156, 157, 158, 167, 170, 173, 176, 181, 184, 190, 193, 196, 206, 211, 214, 218, 229, 232, 239

© Photography by Steven Palowsky: 4, 44

© Photography by Russell A. Graves: 84, 85, 104, 162, 200